music, reading, socializing, traveling, and walking – living a simple, fulfilling life in what she affectionately calls her "Blue Zone," a region where people live longer and healthier lives due to their lifestyle and environment.

Advanced Praise For Finding Joy

"Joy Fox has led a deeply brave and adventurous life. And those adventures began at a very young age. This first volume of Joy's memoir, which starts in 1930s England at a pivotal point in history and takes you through her family's journey to a new life in Canada and her early years as a newlywed, is a beautifully written and deeply inspirational, historical coming-of-age account of a young life spent embracing the unknown and living boldly. It is a must-read for women everywhere who want to live their lives without being defined by inhibitions. And it leaves you eager to read what comes next for Joy Fox in her endlessly fascinating life."

- Mia Taylor, award-winning journalist and travel writer.

FINDING JOY

MY LIFE BEGAN WHEN
I PAWNED THE RING

JOY ELISE FOX

CANADA
www.epictalesmedia.com

Table of Contents

Dedicated to my Mother
MARGERY (MADGE) LILIAN STAFF
1899-1975

Joy Fox's mother at age 16 in 1916.

Part I: Early Years
1935-1943

WAR YEARS, LIFE BEFORE EMIGRATION

Introduction

Adventures are ageless

I turned 90 in October 2025 and celebrated this significant milestone amidst the breathtaking landscapes of Iceland. My life has been a dynamic journey of discovery, resilience, and growth. Every trip I have taken has been more than just exploring new places – it has been about discovering more about myself, uncovering strengths I didn't realise I possessed, and growing stronger because of those experiences. Reflecting back, I see that some of the most important lessons come from embracing the unknown and trusting that we can grow regardless of our age. Here's to continuing that journey.

My beginnings were humble, born into a family in England, where I faced extreme hardships during and after WWII. Despite these challenges, my mother's unwavering belief in my potential instilled in me resilience and a fiery determination. Over time, I managed to achieve most of my goals, though finding and using my voice was a slow and often painful process. Nonetheless, my experiences over the years taught me the profound freedom that comes from handling whatever life throws your way.

I have learned that our most valuable lessons often come from moments of adversity. In 1970, just before the birth of my third child, life once again threw me a curveball, leaving me no choice but to rely on myself. This challenging experience helped me discover a fierce independence that has carried me through to today.

My love for travel blossomed early. Before turning 21, after nursing a broken heart from a broken engagement, I sold a beautiful heirloom engagement ring – a decision born of fear but also resolve – and planned a trip to Italy. Though anxious, I was eager to escape gossip and heartbreak back home. That trip ignited a lifelong passion for exploring the world. I returned feeling stronger, more confident, and more determined to keep exploring because if I could do that, I could do anything.

Shortly after my first adventures abroad in Italy, I found myself in a situation where I had to stand up for myself, slugging a man who tried to assault me. That boldness carried over into my career, where I learned to boldly ask for a raise and refused to fetch cigarettes for a male coworker. I also sought and found a better-paying job to help my family save for our planned move to Canada in 1958. These steps made me feel stronger, and I knew that believing in myself was key to making it happen.

Traveling solo became a way to confront my fears, and although I still feel nervous before each trip, I go anyway and remind myself of my first ever adventure in Italy. In 2024, I was honoured to receive a solo travel award in recognition of the founder of JourneyWoman, Evelyn Hannon, which led to a viral BBC article and further publicity.

Later, when my family settled in Quebec, I realised I didn't share much in common with the local Anglo community, who played golf and cards. Instead, I chose to embrace the French culture, learning the language, choosing a French doctor, and building relationships with the welcoming Québécois. That decision to embrace and integrate into the local culture has become a core value of mine to always promote a sense of belonging, openness, and respect wherever I am situated.

By my 60s, I had climbed the corporate ladder successfully but still felt unfulfilled in my career. I decided to reinvent myself – training at the Protocol School of Washington, gaining certifications, launching a business, and founding a Canadian association of independent meeting planners in 1996, now known as CanSPEP (Canadian Society of Professional Event Planners). I was truly surprised and delighted when CanSPEP established the Joy Fox Award for Vision, Innovation, and Leadership at their 10th anniversary. Over the years, my efforts received recognition – awards, media coverage, and the satisfaction of creating something meaningful.

Art has played a significant role in my life. I've painted for many years, selling a few pieces and notecards, and I still enjoy painting scenes from my travels. Writing has been a constant companion – penning articles, two e-books – *Knitting on the Road Less Ravelled* and *The Cat that Quacked*, and dreaming of resurrecting an unpublished manuscript titled *Knitting Inspirations from the Garden*. Indeed, gardening has been my sanctuary in spring and summer, offering both work and peaceful observation, as well as a source of relaxation and renewal.

My early memories as a child evacuee during WWII deeply influenced my love of beauty and colour. After my father left us, my brothers and I were permitted to evacuate with our mother to escape the German bombing of England. It was a tumultuous and traumatic time. I often found solace sitting on the stairs of the new home where we stayed with strangers, secretly studying the vibrant wallpaper. These rich colours helped me make sense of the chaos and uncertainty surrounding me, fueling my lifelong passion for beauty, art, and vivid hues in my fashion and home decor. Since then, I have filled each home with vibrant shades, cultivated beautiful gardens bursting with colourful flowers alongside my husband, and always used colour as a means of expression.

From a young age, I discovered that my passions could unexpectedly become sources of joy and purpose. I was a shy child who was too afraid to speak up in class, and I eventually joined Toastmasters to learn how to speak professionally. Music was my first love, singing in school shows, joining choirs, and being the lead vocalist for a small band in Victoria, B.C., for twenty years. Making a CD was a bucket-list dream, and after completing my first, our band went on to produce several more. I am ever grateful to my mother, who encouraged me to sing as a child and helped me find the confidence to perform in front of others. I sold those CDs at concerts and craft shows, cherishing those moments.

My love for knitting began at four years old when my mother taught me the craft. Today, I still design and create with yarn – no more unpicking matted sweaters, just creating beautiful pieces with fresh yarn. My early involvement in the knitting industry was significant; I attended events, taught locally and on an Alaskan cruise, and sold my work at craft shows. I even wrote industry newsletters, which deepened my passion and connection to this art.

Moving to Vancouver Island in Western Canada thirty years ago marked a transformative chapter in my life. Here, I embraced the idea of living in a 'Blue Zone,' places where people thrive into their hundredth year. These years on the island have taught me valuable lessons about embracing the unknown and trusting in growth at any age.

Life has also presented challenges along the way. When my husband was diagnosed with Parkinson's disease and eventually passed away, I cared for him until the very end. I am grateful to be surrounded by caring friends and neighbours, who have supported me through difficult times. Today, I embrace life here by volunteering, writing, and living with purpose.

I never imagined I'd still be here, outliving most of my immediate family. Overcoming a difficult childhood taught me resilience; I refused to let the past define my future. Instead, I focused on growth through reading, learning, and striving to improve every day. I am grateful that I can speak openly about my experiences and embrace my story. It wasn't until I reviewed Ben Wicks's book 'The Day They Took the Children,' about WWII child evacuees, and saw my story featured in reviews in national newspapers, that I began to speak more openly about my memories. Wicks used my story in his second book on the topic, 'Nobody Said Goodbye,' which motivated me to share my childhood experiences more freely.

Subsequently, I traveled to the UK to trace my journey from birth to emigration. By that time, I knew discussing my past wouldn't trigger negative thoughts but instead helped me come to terms with everything. Writing about my story became a form of liberation; I gave myself that gift on my 65th birthday. My freedom came from being true to myself. I am eager to share this gift of writing about my childhood in this memoir, with a second book about my experiences in Canada soon to follow.

Today, I cherish the woman I've become. The little girl inside me endured many adversities and trials, but she's no longer lonely and living peacefully, grateful for every challenge overcome. Now at ninety, I refuse to be defined by my age, and my heart remains youthful. Each day, I live with joy, intention, and gratitude, fully embracing life's vibrant possibilities.

Love,
Joy Elise Fox
October 2025
Vancouver Island

Foreword

I grew up knowing my mother through the eyes and mind of a child. She was the woman who made my lunches, sent me off to Sunday school, reminded me to wear a proper coat, and insisted that I 'sit up straight'. I fondly remember the days when we sat together watching our black and white TV, hung out on the sun-laden patio with our dogs Shaney and Foxy and traveled on hockey trips in Canada and even abroad to England and beyond.

But as I got older, I realized I knew far less about who my mother was and where her inner strength came from. I certainly had never fully understood the girl she used to be before she met my father.

This book changed that.

In these pages, I came to know a young woman growing up in England during one of the most turbulent chapters of modern history. I also came to know how she was raised by her own mother, Madge, who was stronger in spirit and morale than my maternal grandfather – who was a combination of philandering Freemason and Pipe Major in the Royal Scots. I also came to know someone who had lost siblings before her birth and during the war, a cruel reminder of how difficult a time that was. I discovered the quiet but unshakeable courage forged in my mother by the air-raid sirens of World War II, by nights spent in shelters, and by the everyday uncertainty that defined her generation. These weren't necessarily polished lessons or moral tales; they were lived experiences that were raw, unfiltered, and formative.

But what surprised me the most was not just her endurance, but her courage. Imagine being a young woman in the post-war years, handed an engagement ring by a boyfriend who later decided he wanted it back. Most people would have meekly complied, returned it, and carried on with their lives as it was. Not my mother. She pawned the ring, used the money to board a ship, and set off, alone, to see a world of which she'd only dreamed.

That story, both the grit of wartime England and the spark of a woman determined to shape her own fate, feels incredibly necessary and modern. And beyond getting to know my mother through a different time, perhaps this book matters more in our current context. We live in a world obsessed with challenging independence, promoting upside-down conformance and squeezing personal agency. Yet here is a story, my mother's story, that pushes up against these values and breaks through the door that many can't get through.

Her story feels necessary right now.

Through this book, I met someone I wished I had known earlier. Someone brave enough to uproot herself, curious enough to explore the unknown, and stubborn enough to follow her own compass even when the world pushed her to think and do otherwise. This book is not just a chronicle of her past; it is an invitation for all of us, especially this current generation, to remember that extraordinary lives are often made from ordinary beginnings, and that courage doesn't always roar. Sometimes, it's a young woman pawning a ring and stepping onto a ship.

I am proud to share my mother's story with you. I hope, as you read, you come to know her as I have: not just as a mother or grandmother or a woman from another era, but as a remarkable human being whose journey deserves to be remembered and celebrated.

Steve Fox

Prologue

The Beginning: Another baby girl in Scotland in 1935

Ouch – what the heck was that? I was being pushed through a slippery tunnel, completely dark, feeling scared to leave the warmth of my hiding place.

Make it stop, my head hurt like crazy.

I couldn't speak or cry; my eyes were closed, and the tunnel was closing in more and more. All I wanted was for it to end.

I could feel my head becoming pointed as I slid along, so narrow and confining.

Then suddenly, everything felt different; something had changed.

I was sliding faster now, and then my head burst out of the end of that tunnel, followed by my body, and I skidded onto something soft.

I was so mad and scared that I opened my mouth and screamed at the top of my lungs. I waved my arms and hollered my outrage – wow, that experience was just nasty.

I didn't know where I was, but I was slimy and dirty – ugh.

Something soft, wet, and warm was on my face. It didn't hurt, but it felt so nice after that shock of racing through the dark tunnel.

Someone leaned over and, with big shears, cut a blue tube coming out of my navel.

A blanket was wrapped around me, pinning my arms to my chest.

I couldn't even move my arms to protest. That made me even angrier. My mouth still worked, so I used it to scream some vulgar baby language.

What a trip! That felt like being shot out of a cannon. Now I had to figure out where I was. One minute I was resting quietly in a warm pool, and the next I was hurtling through a dark tunnel.

Then I heard a quiet voice say, "You have a baby girl."

Ah, so now life begins. I calmed down a little, curious to see what would happen next.

This feels like a new beginning; life?

So, this is it, who knew?

Here I was, waiting to see what was next.

Welcome to the world, me.

A pretty blonde woman, just after giving birth, lay in bed, exhausted after delivering her sixth child. Her hair was limp and damp with sweat, and her body still bore the swelling from labour. She was 35 years old, and this was her sixth baby.

Tears of happiness welled up as she thought, "My third girl, please, God, let her survive." Yet, a wave of sadness washed over her as she remembered the two baby girls she had lost: Marjorie at just three days old, and Muriel Joyce at three months. They were always with her, buried deep in her heart. One of them was buried in a place she couldn't visit.

Her hope was renewed with this third girl. She decided to name her Joy, reflecting the feelings swelling within her. She closed her eyes, whispering a silent prayer for her baby's health and survival. Her prayers were answered. I would go on to celebrate my 90th birthday, outliving everyone in my immediate family.

My mother, Madge, was blessed with three healthy boys – my brothers. The eldest son was Colin, born in 1925 in Colchester, the town where Madge lived, and where she had married. George Greenfield, a Pipe Major in the Royal Scots, was stationed in Colchester, a military town in Essex, England. Mum was born in 1899 and married George in 1924.

When George, my father, was posted to Quetta, India, my mother and their firstborn son Colin went with him. It was during this time in Quetta that she tragically lost her first daughter, Marjorie, who was born prematurely and lived only three days. Despite this loss, my mother was already pregnant again when George was transferred once more, this time to China, where he was stationed in Peking (now Beijing). There, my brother Ian Cameron was born in 1928. His birthplace appearing on his passport caused him numerous problems later in life, as China was a communist country. He was frequently questioned at border controls, and these issues persisted throughout his life, highlighting how early circumstances can have lasting impacts.

My father was then transferred to another British military station in Egypt. Aside from losing her baby in India, it was a novelty for mum, who was not accustomed to having local Indian servants, to be waited upon and addressed as

'Memsahib,' a title for a white foreign woman of high social standing.

When my father was transferred back to Scotland in 1932, my mother was pregnant again. Muriel was born in 1933 but only lived for three months. Mum and Dad, along with Colin and Ian, settled into military housing at Penicuik Barracks, just outside Edinburgh. Alan Neal Gordon was born in August 1934. I was the third baby girl, born barely a year later, in October 1935.

Mum and dad had four children who were alive and healthy, but their marriage was strained. My father was not exactly a kind man – I'm being honest here – he was quite the character, a bit of a ladies' man. He had many affairs and was quite insistent on having sex frequently. He didn't believe in contraception, so mum often found herself pregnant again before she had fully recovered from the last birth.

Despite all this, mum loved him deeply, even though she knew he was something of a rogue. My father, a true Scot, famously did not wear underpants beneath his kilt – something I'd prefer not to explain how I know. Their marriage lasted ten years, during which time she gave birth to six children.

Before World War II broke out, my father was transferred several times; first to Wraysbury, then to Staines, and later to Ashford. He was hired to teach Scottish Country Dancing, Sword Dancing, and Bagpipes to an organization of girl pipers. Unfortunately, he found it too tempting to keep his hands to himself around the girls, and he was eventually asked to leave that job.

Shortly after we moved to Ashford, Middlesex in 1938, my father left my mother. He had a girlfriend in London and moved in with her, leaving mum alone with four children at a time when war was looming on the horizon.

I was just four years old when World War II started in 1939. Ashford is situated near where Heathrow Airport was later built, close to London City, which meant our area experienced heavy bombing during the war.

An Anderson shelter or bomb shelter had been built in our garden, a necessary protection from enemy air raids in the face of the looming war. It became our refuge, as well as for our neighbours. We would go on to spend countless nights inside that shelter, clutching each other in the darkness. When the sirens sounded during the day, we would hurriedly escape to our safe haven.

During this tense time, my father was living with his 'mistress.' She eventually bore him six children. Mum refused to divorce him, although she often had to take him to court because he refused to support us, his four children with her.

Meanwhile, in Ashford, the boys headed off to school each morning, their figures waving goodbye as they walked along the road. I watched them go, feeling a mix of pride and worry.

My mother faced many hardships in the years that followed. Yet, for our sake, she remained strong and resolute, guiding us through some of the darkest days. Now, I often find myself yearning for her presence, wishing she could have experienced more joyful moments in her later years.

CHAPTER 1

Middlesex

The haunting wail of bagpipes drifted from the parade down Main Street, a soulful melody that always stirred something deep within me. I remember standing there, looking up at my father leading the procession, his pride shining through as he walked at the front, a Pipe Major in the Royal Scots.

I didn't really know him, not beyond those early childhood years. He was only present until I was about three. When mum met him in her hometown of Colchester, he was stationed at the army barracks, a fixture in that garrison town. My mother grew up in Colchester with her parents, Charles and Julia Staff, her sister Rose, and her brothers Sid and Ernie.

It's easy now to see why a young woman like mum would have been captivated by the sight of a dashing Pipe Major in full regalia. His uniform must have been nothing short of striking – kilt, sporran, shining insignia – all topped with bagpipes slung over his shoulder. Watching him lead that parade, surrounded by the echoing pipes, must have seemed like a storybook scene. She fell in love with him, and when she was 24, they married.

My earliest memories are of those regal parades with mum and my brothers lining the roadside, faces turned toward my father. The sounds of those pipes still make me cry, even now. It's the first image I have of him. How I loved the sound of the bagpipes. They have always given me chills, filling my mind with their mournful, beautiful sound; despite the bittersweet feelings they bring, intertwined with my father's fleeting presence in my life.

When mum married George Greenfield, they spent their honeymoon in Norwich, Norfolk. My father was stationed in Colchester for a year after their wedding, and it was there that their first child, Colin, was born in 1925. Following that, his military assignments took them to Quetta, India, and Beijing, China.

Joy's parents' wedding photo in August 1924. Joy's mother, Madge, holds the bouquet while Joy's father, George, is dressed in his military uniform.

Joy's mother Madge with baby Colin in 1925.

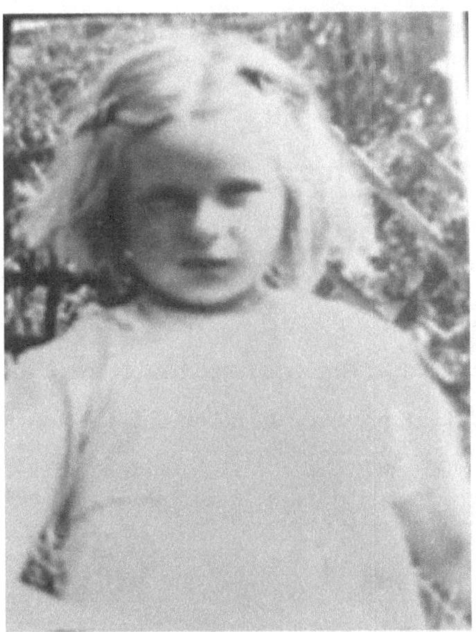

Joy at age 3 in 1938.

Around 1928, while living in Beijing, mum took a walk with baby Ian in a pram and a toddler Colin by her side. Without warning, she wandered into the Forbidden City, which was the former imperial palace for emperors for more than 500 years, and was promptly chased out by guards bearing bayonets. That was one of many stories my mother told us about her travels abroad with our father. She often reminisced about riding in carriages pulled by Tonga horses in India. These horses had a peculiar habit of farting a lot while pulling the carts, and any strange smell from then on was quickly associated with Tonga horses.

My father's career then took him to Egypt for a short spell before returning to Scotland in 1933, where the Royal Scots barracks were located in Penicuik, Edinburgh. That same year, Mum was pregnant with Muriel Joyce, who was born in 1933 but sadly lived only three months. She is buried in Scotland. A year later, in 1934, Alan Neal Gordon was born in August. I joined the family in October 1935, the same year that Elvis Presley was born. By this time, mum had given birth to six children. We lived first in Staines-on-Thames, then Wraysbury.

In 1936, my father was transferred to another area to train the local female piping group in bagpipes, sword dancing, and Scottish country dancing. According to stories mum told us, he couldn't keep his hands off the girls, so he was eventually moved to Ashford, Middlesex. It was from there that I watched him in parades and around the house. My earliest memories begin in those days.

My father was with us for a very brief period in our lives. His departure left a lasting void, as he chose to reject mum and us, his children, in favour of living with Lily in London, another woman he had met along the way. Eventually, he fathered six children with Lily and built a new life with another family.

The only clue that mum ever offered as to why he abandoned us was his inability to be trusted around young girls, an issue exemplified by his affairs with the girl pipers. He once wanted me to live with him, but my mother, ever vigilant, refused. I'm grateful she was so watchful – I was only three at the time, after all.

In 1939, shortly after he had abandoned us, World War II broke out. The shadow of war seemed to stretch over everything, adding chaos to our already turbulent lives.

I always felt that mum never fell out of love with my father. For her, that love was eternal. She used to say my father was a womanizer, and I only knew that he treated her badly for the rest of her life. Despite the pain, she never divorced him, even when opportunities arose later in her life to remarry. She believed that staying married to him was a punishment for his sins, but in truth, it was a punishment that she inflicted upon herself. She often had to take him to court to force him to pay child support, which left her feeling bitter and resentful towards my father and distrustful of men.

My father was a Freemason, a member of the world's oldest fraternal organization that traces its origins back to the local fraternities of stonemasons in the late Middle Ages. This secret male-only group provided support and fellowship to its members. Interestingly, some of the male judges in the courts mum had to appear in were also Freemasons. It seemed to explain why he was often excused from paying child support.

She would relentlessly hound him for what was owed, believing that the old boys' club was still alive and well, working in his favour. As a single mother, she stood little chance against such powerful networks.

When we lived in Ashford, Middlesex, life was a challenge for my mum, looking after my three brothers and me. The two older boys attended the local school. Alan, at age four, attended a nearby kindergarten, while Ian and Colin went to community schools. Ian was bright and passed an exam to go to a grammar school, but refused because he was afraid of the bullies. The bullies seemed drawn to gentle and sensitive boys like him, already vulnerable due to our family situation and our poverty.

Every morning, I watched as my brothers headed off to school, wishing desperately to go with them. But when I eventually joined them, I hated it. To my utter shock, girls and teachers often proved to be bullies too, and the schoolyard was a horrific battlefield I was never prepared for.

Since there were no other little girls nearby, I spent endless hours playing with Corky, our neighbour's cat. She became my best friend, and spending time with her made me feel less lonely.

Corky was a tortoiseshell cat, a wonderfully undemanding playmate, and I loved her dearly. She was a very special cat. I remember how she would allow me to dress her up in tiny bonnets and dresses. She loved being cuddled like a baby and enjoyed being pushed around in my little tin pram.

The pram was navy blue with a delicate white line painted along the side. It had large wheels and a long, curved handle that I could barely reach. I loved being pushed in it, especially when mum had the time to push me up and down the street. As a small child, I fit snugly inside, knees raised to my chin, arms clasped around them, while mum pushed me, gallantly and patiently.

While being pushed, I would often close my eyes and pretend I was a baby again. I loved the smell of the pram's interior and the faint, musty scent from the compartment beneath where I kept my little treasures: a toy soldier that belonged to Ian with his set of tiny dice in a wooden bottle, and a tiny wooden shoe, probably a gift from mum.

I never had a doll, so Corky became my furry doll, my first faithful companion. Our garden had a curved Anderson shelter made of steel sheets, and sometimes Corky and I would play inside of it during the day. I was initially afraid to go in, but Corky, full of natural curiosity, would walk right in without hesitation. She explored on tiptoe, sniffing everything – blankets, old clothes, crumbs, dirt – and would curl up on a makeshift bed, only her tiny pink nose poking out as I covered her up.

Corky was a darling in every way. Since her, I haven't found another cat that allowed me to dress them up or shared such a close bond. She was truly unique, my first furry friend. Sometimes, I could tempt her into the kitchen for breakfast or lunch. She loved cheese and milk, and I loved watching her ears twitch, always alert to any scraps she might get.

That was when my love for cats truly began. Corky's unique 'cattitude' made her the perfect companion for a lonely child, a dear and irreplaceable friend. Through Corky, I discovered that genuine friendship and curiosity can transform the simplest moments into lifelong memories. True friends accept us as we are, with all our quirks and passions, and they brighten our world just by being part of it.

CHAPTER 2

The Shelter

I pulled the pillow over my head to shut out the relentless sound of the planes going by overhead. We knew they were enemy bombers, their immense bodies slicing through the sky with a menacing droning that we had come to dread. It was an awful, constant noise that seemed to seep into our very bones, making our hearts pound in fear. When the planes passed overhead, without the terrifying whistle of a bomb, relief washed over us, especially while huddled in our bomb shelter.

The war began in 1939, when I was only four years old, and from that moment on, every night was a test of our courage and patience. During the intense days of the Blitz in 1940-41, hundreds of bombs rained down on England. The air raids and the distant explosions brought fear and destruction, and it was unsettling to know that somewhere not too far away, lives were being upended, homes reduced to rubble, and families torn apart.

The shelter was made of corrugated iron and compacted soil, had no windows, only a tunnel leading into the earth, and was covered with coarse sacking to muffle the roar of enemy planes overhead. I remember the suffocating, damp smell of concrete and earth, which seemed to seep into my bones, fuelling my fears of being buried alive beneath the rubble.

We became familiar with the ominous German Doodlebugs, alien in appearance and sound. Their distinctive whistling warned us of impending doom – the terror of hearing that whistle and knowing what was coming struck deep into my young and impressionable heart.

As the droning noise of the Doodlebug sounded, I would hold my breath, silently hoping it would pass us by without damage. When I finally released the pillow to track the sound, my heart pounded so loudly I feared it might give me away. Panicking, I strained my ears to catch the engine's stopping sound; an indication that the missile had either missed or was gone. When it continued on its deadly path, mum would softly say, "Now children, let's try and get some sleep, shall we?" It was a lesson in resilience, a reminder that amid fear and destruction, we had to find small moments of calm.

These experiences taught me more about bravery than I ever expected at such a young age. In the face of overwhelming danger, there is strength in unity, in leaning on each other and holding onto hope. The war profoundly shaped me: it helped me develop perseverance and compassion. I grew up with a quiet determination to never forget those lessons and to treasure peace and safety.

Our immediate neighbours shared the shelter with us. Mr. and Mrs. Short and their beloved cat, Corky, who had become a very dear friend to me. Mrs. Short was always careful to keep Corky with her, especially during air raids, because she didn't want Corky to be alone in the house or in the garden. She knew how frightened Corky would be if a bomb fell nearby. So, Corky was always with us in the shelter. Most of the time, Corky slept with Mrs. Short, but occasionally she would come to me for a cuddle, curling up comfortably in my arms.

Corky took my mind off the war, which to me was loud noises in the night that scared me. She also distracted me from sleeping in a makeshift bed with people who weren't family. I often wondered what the war would bring next. As a child, I couldn't grasp the full meaning of war, but I sensed its danger. It was hard to understand why bombs were falling and being dropped on us. It was difficult for a child to grasp. The why of it all remained a mystery, one that even adults struggled to explain.

Strangers sometimes entered, usually those far from their own shelters, disrupting what little privacy there was. We'd huddle together, feeling a mix of fear and camaraderie, until the all-clear sounded and they left. The adults spoke in hushed tones, their voices trembling as they discussed where the bombs might be falling, each word heavy with dread. We silently mourned those who were dying that night, feeling a strange, numb sorrow and trauma. I learned a little about the different types of bombs used during the war – incendiary, Mills, doodlebugs, the VI – and listened intently, though I couldn't fully understand any of it. All we could do was cling to optimism, praying it would never be our turn to hear the terrible sound of a bomb hurtling towards us.

My mother, the only guardian I knew, bore the weight of it all. Watching her carefully consider every decision for our family made me realise the heavy burdens she carried. I knew she thought about worst-case scenarios and what would happen if our house was hit and if she couldn't protect us. It made me appreciate her even more.

The war was a constant conversation, everyone's concern. My 14-year-old brother, full of bravado, sometimes ignored warnings to go to the shelter, believing himself invincible. One day, a stray piece of shrapnel pierced his bed, startling him into reality. After that, he always stayed in the shelter during the air raids.

I hated the shelter. It became a big part of our lives, and what was a novelty at first quickly became a major nuisance, a disruption of our day-to-day lives. After being hustled out of the warm house, into a cold underground shelter every day or night, it ceased to be fun. It felt like cruelty to be taken from warm to cold and damp. I have no idea how safe the shelters really were, and I thought that if a bomb dropped directly on it, we would be buried alive or killed. I worried constantly about that especially in the dark, with the only light coming from flickering candles or the faint glow of the shelter's entrance.

We called the air raid siren "Moaning Minnie" because its mournful sound seemed to broadcast our fears. The silence after the all-clear was a moment of relief, when we could cautiously emerge, creep around, and breathe again. Many towns had above-ground street shelters, concrete boxes with a flat roof and a narrow doorway, built to protect civilians who could not reach their home shelters in time if they were out and about when the siren sounded. After the war, they became dark, musty playgrounds for children to play hide and seek, and reeked of urine and feces; and sometimes, they were a convenient meeting place for quick romantic encounters.

During the war, subway or tube stations served as shelters, with many families camping on the platforms and along the tracks. Privacy was secondary; safety was the main concern. Later in the war, we had a Morrison shelter, a sturdy iron table, inside our home. It was an unforgiving piece of furniture designed to protect us during the worst bombings, and it was big enough for the family to huddle under together. It replaced our dining table. The sides were heavy mesh panels. The inside could be made as comfortable as possible with a mattress, pillows and blankets.

Although the war was a harrowing experience, it shaped my outlook on life and taught me about the resilience of the human spirit and the importance of kindness. I came to value my mother's steadfast strength and the importance of community and compassion in crises.

CHAPTER 3

Homeless

The Blitz of World War II is widely considered one of the worst times for civilians in England during the war. London endured an escalating wave of relentless bombing, which caused intense hardship and terror. Every night, the sky lit up with distant explosions, and the tremors of falling bombs shook the city, while their frightening roar echoed through the darkness.

As London faced the unending bombing, the danger extended to the suburbs. We could hear the distant explosions growing louder, closer, each one a terrifying reminder that no one was safe. The darkness outside threatened to overwhelm the fragile security of our lives. Because we lived near what is now Heathrow Airport in a small town called Ashford that was just big enough to have an aerodrome, we caught the brunt of the bombings. London Airport was constructed in 1946, a year after the war ended, and it wasn't renamed Heathrow until 1966.

Unfortunately, we spent an increasing amount of time rushing into the dark, cramped space of the shelters during air raids or sleeping on makeshift bedding. It became an everyday routine seared into my memory. The deafening sound of bombs whistling and exploding around us was haunting.

As we prepared for each new threat, the constant vigilance and shared routines in the shelter became an unspoken part of our lives. Mum had a trunk in the shelter that she used as a makeshift table, filled with essential items we might need if our house were bombed. At night, she would sit on the trunk, her face illuminated by the flickering glow of a candle, and read us stories to soothe our frightened minds. When sleep finally came, it was restless and broken by the piercing 'All Clear' signal; that stark reminder that the danger had passed, at least for now.

Usually, the chilling sound of an air raid warning would send us rushing into the shelter, our hearts pounding. Over time, we grew accustomed to hearing the mournful wail of 'Moaning Minnie' and listening intently for the return of the 'All Clear,' the signal that we could cautiously venture back to our house, praying it had remained unscathed.

Then, on one traumatic, unforgettable night, our house took a direct hit. The impact was deafening, and the house was declared uninhabitable. I couldn't comprehend that a house could not be lived in. Our home was gone in an instant, reduced to rubble and ash. Then the Anderson shelter became our temporary home until the authorities arranged for us to stay in a spare room at someone's house in St. Albans. Many families with houses that had spare rooms were asked to take in evacuees from the bombing areas.

Overnight, we became evacuees, too. More than one million child evacuees were transported by train to live temporarily in the countryside, with a label displaying their name pinned to their coat as they held their small gas masks in a cardboard box.

However, unlike many children who left their parents behind in the cities, we stayed with mum as she was alone and a single mother, a wife abandoned by her husband and now homeless. Her life was further torn apart by the cruelty of war. We were placed in a distant house, farther from the main areas that experienced most of the bombings. I prayed fervently that this new place would keep us safe. Those days felt like a series of upheavals, shock blending into despair and dread.

Despite the chaos surrounding us, we clung desperately to small signs of normalcy. The trunk in the shelter was now open, revealing its hidden treasures. I was curious and looked through it. Mum had packed what she believed to be absolute necessities, carefully choosing items in case we found ourselves in this unexpected situation. She had packed a set of clothes for each of us as an immediate change from our pajamas, which we were wearing. The boys each had a pair of pants; Alan's were short and typical of that time, while Ian's and Colin's were longer. Each boy had a shirt, a sweater, underwear, socks, a jacket, and shoes. I had a simple skirt, a sweater, one pair of underpants, socks, shoes, and a lightweight coat. These were small comforts amid uncertainty.

Mum herself had packed her cherished jar of beads, her one fine dress, turquoise with brown check trims and a pair of brown shoes, a cardigan, woollen stockings, and a coat. She also included two of her evening dresses from her days as an Officer's wife: one was a pink net tube with frills cascading down the skirt; the other, a daring purple satin dress with a bare shoulder and a plunging low back. Both stunning, yet impractical. Her dancing shoes completed her carefully selected ensemble. I realized later how impractical these evening dresses and dancing shoes were, but they still brought her joy during those difficult days.

Perhaps she yearned for a return to those distant, glamorous days when she had danced in these exquisite dresses in faraway ballrooms. She refused to part with them, and so they traveled with us through the war as a precious reminder of a happier era.

Inside the trunk, alongside her dresses, were her personal papers, photographs, birth certificates, and a small Bible. Inside the Bible's cover, nestled gently, was a withered mask, an odd relic mum said had once covered her face at birth, believed to bring good luck. Yet, that talisman seemed distant from the realities of her life as I knew it, a symbol of hopes and superstitions in a life turned upside down.

There was also a Chinese shawl in the trunk, black with a long fringe and covered in intricate red embroidery depicting dragons and flowers. I kept it in my own trunk for many years, a silent keeper of memories, before passing it on to one of my girls. When we finally opened the trunk, we dressed ourselves and carefully packed the pajamas inside, momentarily forgetting about the bombs and the hardships of war.

We then settled into the dark shelter, a temporary refuge that offered little comfort but a sense of safety. We waited anxiously for someone, most likely a warden, to arrive, to evaluate the destruction and determine who had been hurt.

During those bleak days, as evacuees torn from our home, we were entirely vulnerable and dependent on the kindness of strangers for our basic needs and a place to live. With four children to care for and feed, and with no regular income, mum was filled with worries about our future and still haunted by the heartbreak of our father's abandonment. That ache of our father's absence was still raw in our hearts.

I cannot imagine how my mother must have felt, carrying so much pain silently, her strength tested at every turn, amid so much upheaval. Yet she put on a brave face and a smile for her children; a survivor's and mother's instincts. She graciously supported us with a kind word, a reassuring touch, and a hug. She was the pillar of strength that kept us from being utterly consumed by darkness.

CHAPTER 4

Evacuees at 17 College Road, St. Albans

When the air-raid wardens came around to our shelter, we were quickly transported by bus to a small house on College Road at St. Albans. It felt like a world away from the chaos of London's bombing raids, offering a rare instance of peace and calm. We were crammed into one spare bedroom, the only place we could call our own during those uncertain days. We weren't allowed to enter the other rooms or use the bathroom, and the owners of the house were complete strangers who kept their distance from us. They had children, but we weren't allowed to play or mingle with them. Everything we needed to do had to happen in that tiny room.

My eldest brother, Colin, was old enough to enlist, so he joined the Fleet Air Arm. I remember how proud and handsome he looked, wearing his uniform when he came home on leave. It was hard to see him go, knowing he was risking so much.

Living in that small, single room was a challenge, a real test of patience, often pushing me to my limits. Mum was allowed to draw water from the house owner's bathroom for us, and she had to empty our makeshift toilet bucket into their toilet. Every day, we washed ourselves with a shared bowl of water. Mum did her best to lift our spirits so that we wouldn't get discouraged by the bleak living conditions. She pulled out a jar of beads from the trunk, and together we threaded them onto a string to make privacy curtains. They only offered a tiny bit of separation, but it was something.

I loved sitting quietly on the stairs, watching the stained-glass panel in the front door. The patterns changed with the weather outside, rays of sunlight or grey clouds casting shifting colours on the walls. Even though I wasn't supposed to be there on the staircase, I couldn't resist gazing and losing myself in those fleeting, beautiful images.

The first house Joy and her family were evacuated to on College Road in St. Albans in 1941. Joy captured this photo during her visit to England in 2000.

During this time, mum and dad became legally separated. Dad wanted custody of us, but mum fought fiercely to keep us together. She was awarded custody, especially since he had abandoned us during the war. He was supposed to pay child support regularly, but he didn't. Only after mum dragged him to court multiple times did he pay her half the amount. It seemed clear that he didn't care much about us. Sometimes he just sent a little money to avoid trouble.

He kept asking for a divorce, but mum refused. She never divorced him, though he continued to have children with his mistress, which made the mess of our family even more complicated. His words could be cruel, and he was often verbally abusive. Mum called him a beast, perhaps an unfair word, but later I understood why she felt that way. I wish I had asked her to explain more, but I was already beginning to realize how harsh and unkind he could be.

One aspect of my father that always stood out to me was his deep interest in history. During the time my parents spent in China, he immersed himself in researching the atrocities of the Chinese Revolution. He kept a scrapbook filled with photographs taken during those turbulent days. There were photos of beheadings, severed heads left on poles along the streets, for all to see. I believe this book must have been in the trunk that we brought to our new place; otherwise, I would not have seen it. The brown sepia photographs depicted heads rolling after being chopped off with a sword. Many prisoners were tortured.

One of the tortures was called the death of a thousand cuts. One piece of flesh was taken at regular intervals from various areas of the body. The scrapbook had a photograph of a prisoner who had been tortured in this manner. He was being held up by two Chinese soldiers, his body a mass of deep gouges arranged in patterns, a circle on each breast area, ovals on his thighs, elongated oblongs on his shins and arms. There was a large circle where his stomach and midriff would have been. Incredibly, he was still alive, thin to the point of starvation, eyes etched with pain. I imagined there were similar patterns on his back.

I wasn't sure why these hauntingly gruesome photos didn't turn my stomach. As a child, I felt like they opened a dark window into something I shouldn't see, yet I couldn't look away. I somehow knew they revealed the wickedness humans are capable of, terrible acts that no child should witness. But my curiosity, stubborn and insatiable, pulled me closer, urging me to face the unsettling truth lurking in those images, as if understanding might somehow make it less frightening. Through this experience, I came to see that facing uncomfortable truths is essential for genuine compassion and personal growth. I believe I learned that empathy isn't just a feeling but a deliberate effort to understand others, which fuels the pursuit of a more just and equitable world.

The trunk was a curious thing, holding not just old clothes but also a small treasure trove of my father's oddities, including an entire Charles Dickens collection, worn but cherished, and some brass ornaments from Egypt, India, and China, each with a story I couldn't quite grasp yet. These belonged to my dad, and I often wondered if one day, he'd come knocking, demanding they be returned. Mum had her own keepsake, a book called The Wide, Wide World, that still sits on my shelf, a quiet link to her.

Mum was like a delicate, beautiful rose, innocent and kind, who had fallen for a man with a roguish smile. She often spoke softly about her lost babies and the simpler, happier days she once knew. I've always secretly wished the two sisters I never knew but imagined – so lively and warm – had lived. They'd have been good company, a gentle buffer against my three brothers, who seemed to live to tease and trouble me.

Our little family found it hard to settle into the small, unfamiliar room. It was clear from the tense silence of the owners of the house that we weren't exactly welcome there. The owners didn't want us, but honestly, we didn't want to be there either. Our toilet was just a bucket in the corner of the bedroom. Mum would fill it with water and empty it when it got too smelly or after we used it, which made everything feel even more temporary.

I'd watch the boys standing up to pee, brave and carefree, while I squatted, feeling both shy and a bit proud of my quiet independence. We stayed in that cramped place for a few months as Alan began attending school, and I was supposed to go to a nursery. With nothing much to do in that single room, I clung to thoughts of going to school. It seemed like a new adventure, a chance to distract myself from our strange, unsettled and disrupted life.

Then came the day we had to leave. The owners, like many before them, complained about us, about tenants who stayed too long. So, we were forced to find somewhere else, another room, another chance. As evacuees, placed in a stranger's spare bedroom, we didn't really have to do anything wrong for us to be kicked out. It was just how things worked. The owners wanted their space back.

And so, the next place we stayed promised to be even worse – another nightmare waiting to happen.

CHAPTER 5

A Sweet Revenge

One day, my mother gently told me I would need to spend a few hours at a nearby nursery school while she figured out how to bring in some money for our family. That moment stayed with me, the quiet resolve in her voice, the fear in her eyes, and the uncertain future before us. I could feel her anxiety in my entire being. After my father left us, life felt stripped to the bare bones; we had almost nothing left and struggled to get by each day. Mum hadn't worked during her marriage, and now, with me still at home, finding a job seemed impossible. She had no formal skills, only her knitting, piano playing, and a quiet determination to build a better, happier life.

I knew she longed for her old dreams of music, a piano in a warm room where she could lose herself in melodies. She had taken lessons as a girl and had dreamed of becoming a musician, but her parents couldn't afford to support her ambitions further. That longing for music stubbornly remained in her heart and could not be extinguished by a failed marriage or the hardships of war.

The nursery school was not far from our temporary home. I remember walking with mum through the quiet town streets, feeling a mix of nervousness and fear of abandonment. She walked me to the school hall where I was to spend my first hours away from her, and I could see her shoulders tighten with worry. I was nervous about leaving her side, especially knowing that my brothers, Alan and Ian, wouldn't be close by. They had already been thrown into their own school experiences, with Alan in a different nursery and Ian in a regular school.

I had overheard their conversations about how much they hated school, which made me fear I would feel the same. Colin and Ian had been bullied at their school, and their refusal to attend grammar school after passing the exams had made them targets. Alan, too, was subjected to bullying, though he rarely spoke of it, and I sensed his pain and loneliness behind his silence.

That day, as my mum handed me over to the teacher, tears welled up in my eyes. I was shy and overwhelmed by the unfamiliar surroundings. Looking back, I see how those early experiences of separation and fear shaped my idea of strength. Mum's quiet resolve, her sacrifices, and her unmet dreams stayed with me, teaching me that even in tough times, we can plant seeds for a better future. This understanding has influenced how I handle challenges.

There was a memory from this nursery school that I haven't been able to shake. The teacher lined us up in pairs in the hall, forming a perfect crocodile of children, her stern eyes scanning us with unwavering discipline. We were not allowed to talk with other children. She was very strict, unwavering in her command for absolute silence. We were told that children should be seen and not heard, a phrase that was meant to make us feel even more insignificant.

She handed each of us a piece of paper, about the size of an 8x11 sheet. I was careful to keep this paper perfectly flat, free of wrinkles or creases. Any crease was met with punishment, a strict rule I barely understood but instinctively feared. We had to keep the paper pristine, ready for drawing once we got to our desks in the hall.

Each of us received a tiny, chewed stub of a pencil, about three or four inches long, my own painted in a periwinkle blue colour I hadn't yet learned to name, but have loved this colour all my life. The stub was worn down from countless previous children who chewed on the pencil. I loved that little sliver of a pencil.

As I carefully kept my paper flat, I longed to draw but knew I had to protect my tiny treasure, the pencil. In my eagerness, I tucked it away into my knickers, which were hand-knit and loose, and had no elastic around the legs. They were my only underwear, knitted from the scraps of an old sweater by my mother, made with love.

Suddenly, my tiny pencil slipped out, falling with a soft plop onto the ground. The teacher, with her piercing, sharp eyes, saw the moment. Her reaction was swift and frightening: she halted the line of children, yanked me out by the arm, and crumpled my paper in her rough hand.

In ominous tones, she declared, "You little thief, wait until I get you in the classroom."

I knew this was trouble. It felt like everything simple and innocent was falling apart, unraveling my little world. She dragged me into the classroom, the crocodile of children trailing behind, and in front of all my peers, she sat on a chair, pulled me across her lap, lifted my skirt, pulled down my woolly knickers and spanked my bare bum for all to see. The raw exposure was mortifying. She continued to spank my bare bottom loudly and mercilessly, even as my entire body trembled.

"That's what you get for stealing," she said harshly.

I burst into loud tears. I had never been spanked before, nor since, come to think of it. The shame and fear overwhelmed me, and suddenly, my bladder betrayed me and let loose. I was so frightened, so humiliated, that I peed myself. The wetness spread quickly, soaking my woolly knickers and, to my horror, landing on her skirt as well.

Her anger deepened and she spanked me again, harder this time. She pushed me off her lap, leaving me to pull up my wet, soggy woolly knickers, with tears streaming down my face.

My carefully kept paper was ruined, and the tiny pencil gone – it was taken away. I sat miserably, quiet, drenched in shame and fear, until my mum arrived to collect me. I knew I wouldn't be allowed to draw that day, and I walked home slightly bow-legged, knowing that mum would have to wash and dry my soggy underwear before I could go out again.

That day taught me some harsh lessons about authority and vulnerability. I saw how teachers can be tough, even bully-like, unkind and unforgiving. In that moment of embarrassment, I felt a strange sense of sweet revenge when I peed on her. She was mean and had it coming.

That childhood experience shaped my ideas about fairness and mercy. It was eye-opening to realize that not every adult or authority figure can be trusted. I also learned not to steal anything, like pencils, or wear hand-knit underwear – lessons I still carry with me!

Looking back, that painful memory of that awful teacher was a quiet wake-up call. Sometimes, the lessons that hurt the most are the ones that stay with us and help guide us to do what's right.

CHAPTER 6

Old Man Davey

After living in a small room at St. Albans, our family moved to a house behind the cinema in the same town. The place belonged to a very unkempt, dirty old man, and both his appearance and the house showed signs of neglect. His hair was greasy, his face was grimy and weathered, and his clothing was stained. The house was dishevelled, filled with a persistent stench that seemed to cling to everything, making it heavy and oppressive. It was uncomfortable, yet we managed to squeeze our belongings into one of the cramped bedrooms.

Old Man Davey, as we called him, was an angry, unpleasant man whose frightening hostility made us feel like we were walking on eggshells in his presence. My mother tried repeatedly to keep the peace, but it was no use. He did not want us there. We stayed out of his way as much as possible, only a few days passing before we returned home to find the house locked and the door bolted from the inside. He had shut us out, clearly with no intention of allowing us back in. My mother shouted through the door, her voice edged with desperation, but he remained steadfast in his refusal.

My brothers and I sat on the pavement beside a low wall that bordered what little we could call a garden, although the ugly weeds and neglect gave it a little charm. My mother had to leave us there, cautioning us not to wander off while she went to the Council Office to seek help. It was a humiliating experience to be left partially helpless, the dirt and disdain of that place weighing on us.

Later, she returned with a man and a ladder. The ladder was set against the upstairs window where our belongings were. Miraculously, the window was unlocked. My mother managed to climb in, reaching down to get our trunk, the beaded curtains, even the toilet bucket. She handed down what little food we had, a handful of comics, some pots and pans, and a few pieces of bed linens and clothes. We gathered around our pile of possessions. We also had no choice but to use the old man's garden as a toilet. It was a bitter lesson in humility and made us feel deeply ashamed.

My mother spread a blanket on the ground and told us to sit there until she returned. We were on the pavement, and the old man was watching us from behind his dirty curtains. We could see him creepily observing us. We quietly hoped she would come back soon because that place, with all its filth and hostility, felt like a dangerous trap.

Ian, my older brother, looked at mum with worry in his eyes and asked, "What are we going to do?"

She assured us that someone would find us another place soon. The man from the Council had left after trying to help, going off to find us a new home. All we could do was wait and huddle together under the worn blanket. I felt small and vulnerable. Despite the hopelessness and despair in a storm we couldn't control, there was strength to be found as we stuck together, which bonded us even more. I am not sure how we managed to get through each day, but we persevered against all odds. Adversity can shape us in positive ways if we learn from it, and can give us the strength to endure future hardships.

Old Man Davey's house was the second home to which Joy and her family were evacuated during WWII in 1942. Joy took this photo in 2000.

I remember my mother's quiet strength in moments like these when it felt as though the walls were closing in on us. My uncle Sid's house in St. Albans was just a stone's throw from where we sat on the pavement, yet it might as well have been in another galaxy. He had a wife, Kitty, and a son, Keith, who was always a mischievous boy, whose grin and taunts I knew too well. He went to the same school as Ian and bullied the poor children at their school. They lived in a small three-bedroom house.

My mother made a difficult decision and she swallowed her pride and went to ask her brother for help. She took Alan and me, and left Ian guarding our possessions which were placed on the ground. I can still see her shoulders hunched with shame, her head bowed as she knocked on his door. Uncle Sid answered, a man I sensed was torn. Mum told him we'd been locked out, stranded on the street. His reply was gentle but firm: "Sorry, there was no room." I believe she expected this answer from him.

If he had given us a room, the authorities might think we'd settled, and we'd be stuck there, unable to find another long-term shelter. He also didn't want us living in his house. His wife, Kitty, was cold and dismissive, telling mum to leave and let the Council handle it. Keith's sneer, mouthing "Na, na, na," is burned into my memory. He was cruel. As a family, we hated him then, and I still do.

As we turned away from uncle Sid's house, I saw the slump in mum's shoulders go lower, and I was dismayed by the way her head hung low from desperation and disappointment. She carried the burden of having to ask for help and of being turned away, which I didn't fully understand then, but I do now.

I believe uncle Sid's regret weighed on him long after that day. Many years later, he reached out and wanted to reconcile with our mother, but their former close relationship had been destroyed. Mum remained close to her other brother, Ernie, who lived in Colchester, and her sister, Rose, who lived in Rowhedge, Essex. She kept those connections alive over the years.

The next hours were cold and damp, fear gnawing at us. It was wartime, and children like us weren't supposed to be out on the streets. Mum, ever resourceful, searched for a community shelter where we could spend the night. She took Alan and me with her again, walking through the dark streets until we found a shelter on the next street. Then we walked back to collect Ian, and with all our belongings gathered in trembling hands, we left the hostile Old Man Davey's place behind for good.

After arriving at the new shelter, we tried to find comfort among strangers, but the threat of air raids loomed large. We slept fitfully, always aware of the danger outside. When morning finally came, mum left to tell the Council where we had stayed. She returned shortly after, her face slightly brighter.

"We have a new place," she said softly, with hope and weariness mingling in her voice. "They're coming for us soon. It's not far away."

That small promise was a balm to our battered souls, and it is true, as they say, that it's darkest before the dawn breaks. It's a lesson I still carry with me: endurance, compassion, and the strength to move forward, no matter how difficult the journey.

The Christian Science Reading Room, London Road

Eventually, we were gathered up, our belongings carefully loaded onto a humble barrow, and we set off towards another new address at 66 London Road. The building housed a quiet Christian Science Reading Room on the ground floor, its windows dusty with age. Above it, we were given a room that felt surprisingly spacious, a stark contrast to our previous cramped quarters. It was larger than any room we had known before, with two simple beds. Mum and I shared one, while the two boys shared the other.

We had access to an old, creaking bathroom, where we drew water from a rusty tap. Although we still performed our daily washing in one room, the extra space in this building seemed a luxury, a gift after all we had endured.

Another family of evacuees shared the house, living across the hall. They had a little girl about my age who would come over and play. She was generous, perhaps too much so, as she gave me chicken pox, which I then passed to the boys. Soon, we all shared measles, a reminder of how fragile and interconnected our health and lives were during those times.

Children are often fascinated by their own bodies and how they differ from the opposite sex, yet society deems such curiosity wrong, a taboo to be avoided. I never quite understood why, but I always knew that boys had something unique – a thing attached. I remembered my father, who would stand in front of the fire with no underwear, warming himself, his buttocks exposed to the flames. Even as a toddler, I sensed this was wrong, something I didn't want to see.

Shortly after, my father left us, and he didn't win custody in the battle for me. Thankfully, I was spared from seeing that part of him again, but the image of him, his jewels on display, burned into my memory and filled me with a fear of him.

I had never seen a female's intimate parts, but my new little friend from across the hall was quite worldly; she knew about sex and the strange things bodies could do. She told me about wet dreams, a concept I'd never heard of before. Despite having three big brothers, I knew nothing about boys or what made them different from girls.

This girl's dangerous knowledge about what a penis was truly frightened me. She explained it could stand up straight when excited, that boys could get stiff just by looking at girls, and that at night, such excitement could cause a wet dream, soiled sheets, and embarrassment.

With this newfound knowledge, I looked at my brothers differently, each one suddenly more mysterious and intriguing. I couldn't wait to tell mum what I'd learned and was eager to share my new understanding.

But the girl was soon forbidden to visit. Mum caught her with her knickers down and dress pushed up, a scene that made me wonder about her curiosity, or was there something more sinister behind her knowledge? As I grew older, I thought about her, wondering whether her questions came from innocent curiosity or something darker, and I hoped she was alright.

With no other playmates, I started roaming downstairs to the Reading Room. I'd wander among the quiet shelves, flipping through pages of open books, pressing my nose against the glass of the windows, creating chaos among the folders on display. I resented my loneliness.

One day, I tore some papers in frustration, making a mess like a spoiled child. Fear of punishment or eviction from our humble lodgings crept in. I waited upstairs for a knock, but it never came. The next day, I found my mess tidied, my guilt hidden, and nobody ever knew.

Then came the day mum announced a photograph. It was to be in sepia, the warm, brown-toned pictures of the era, because Colin was coming home on leave. He looked tall and handsome in his Fleet Air Arm uniform, his chest puffed out, his eyes proud. Ian wore his one suit; Alan, in a grey flannel with short trousers, wrinkled from being folded away. I dressed in a brick-colored sweater, a red plaid skirt from charity, and brown cotton lyle stockings, too big and wrinkled. My shoes were black, and I was told to sit with one leg folded under me.

Mum wore her turquoise dress with a brown check collar and trim. None of us smiled; we just stared straight ahead into the camera, frozen in time. Today, that photograph feels like a window back to some of the most difficult years of our lives, when innocence and adversity mingled. I see my mother's drawn and strained face, her stress clearly visible. I cannot fathom how hard it must have been for her, living in uncertainty as a single mother, with the war dragging on. I was always thinking of how to support her and to make her happy.

The official family photo of Joy's mother, Colin, Ian, Alan and Joy in the room above the Christian Science Reading Room in 1943.

Loneliness often pressed heavily on me then, and I longed for Corky, my cat, my first true friend, who had shared so many childhood secrets. I missed her dearly. She was a tiny, purring comfort. I yearned for companionship, for a pet or a doll to fill the silence, to bring some joy to those lonely days.

I was allowed to wander along the road during daylight, but not very far from our lodging. Miserable and lonely, head down, I scuffed my shoes as I walked along, one foot in the gutter and the other on the path. I was so absorbed in self-pity that I barely heard a sound nearby, a tiny cry coming from the doorway of a deserted building. I stopped to listen, curious about what it was. It was such a faint sound, a little mew. I turned to look into the dark doorway. A tiny kitten was crouched in the corner, wet and bedraggled, so small and ginger with big pleading eyes. I knelt down and extended my finger. The kitten licked my finger, so I picked it up and cuddled it. I held it gently against me, and it purred as I stroked it.

I held it close as I hurried back to our room. When I got there, I burst into the room, where my mother was preparing our dinner.

"Mum, mum, look what I found!" I exclaimed.

"Oh dear," she said softly, her voice tinged with a constant unspoken worry beneath her gentle tone. "You know we can't have animals in here."

I remember the way my little heart sank at her words.

I pleaded, my voice trembling, "But mum, you know how I miss Corky. I have no friends. Couldn't we just keep this little kitten here in secret? Nobody needs to know. I'll look after it, and it can have some of my dinner. Please, please, mum, let me keep it."

The thought of losing that tiny bundle of fur, of abandoning it to the cold, uncaring streets, made me cry. I was so afraid, so desperate for love and companionship.

She looked at me, worry now creasing her brow, her mind clearly weighing the impossible choices. Then she pulled me up close in a warm, forgiving hug.

"I know you wanted a doll, Joy," she murmured softly, her voice thick with emotion. "And I know how much you love animals. I wish I could give you everything you want, but we simply don't have the money for a doll right now. If you promise to keep the kitten in this room, to put paper down for it to use as a toilet, and most importantly, to keep it a secret, then you may keep him. But remember, animals aren't toys. They need gentle treatment, proper food, care, exercise, and attention."

Those words sank deep into my young heart and the happiness I felt after hearing them was overwhelming. I clung to the tiny creature, tears of joy streaming down my face, as he purred and licked my chin affectionately. We named him Hurricane, inspired by the courageous British planes that had flown during the war, symbols of patriotism. I fed him scraps of food and tiny saucers of milk, and he dutifully did his business on the newspaper I laid out. He was a beautiful ginger kitten, with bright eyes and a gentle purr that seemed to say everything would be alright. I felt peace and comfort instantly whenever I cuddled him.

We stayed there until late 1942. Mum often missed her family terribly. One day, she wrote a letter to her sister Rose in Rowhedge, Essex, asking if we could come and live with them. When Rose responded with a warm yes, we began making our plans to leave.

When the day arrived to leave the Christian Science Reading Room, Hurricane came along with us. He was nestled in a bag I carried, his cute little head peeking out, as we walked to find a new home with aunty Rose, uncle Charlie, their eight lively children, a grandson, and our granny. Corky had been my first feline friend, but Hurricane became my second, and somehow, each one left a mark on my soul. My life was forever changed by the animals I loved, both cats and dogs. They taught me vital lessons of unconditional love and gentle patience, values I carry with me even now, at ninety years old, as I reflect on a childhood filled with extreme suffering but also beauty and love.

CHAPTER 7

Country Cousins

Our family moved once more, this time to my Aunt Rose's home in 1942, when I was just six and a half years old. The world was a tumult of chaos and uncertainty, and I was too young to grasp the full weight of it. My brother Alan, ever the elder at seven, and Ian, at thirteen, carried burdens I couldn't yet understand. Colin was still serving in the Fleet Air Arm, far away in a war that disrupted and shaped the very fabric of our lives.

With all our belongings packed into a battered trunk, we boarded the train to Rowhedge. I remember that Hurricane, a tiny, fragile creature in a small bag, also sensed our anticipation. He was a good kitten, innocent and trusting during the upheaval.

When we arrived at Rowhedge station, the air was filled with the scent of metal and lingering engine fumes. We made our way along winding paths to Heath Road, where aunty

Rose's family lived. Their small rented three-bedroom Council house stood modest and worn, yet it held the promise of safety, however temporary.

Back then, to secure a Council House, you had to apply and add your name to a long list and then wait for a chance that might never come quickly enough. Homes would go to those who needed them the most. Life was a constant waiting game in those years. Sometimes, when I'm quiet, I ponder how those difficult childhood days planted the seeds of perseverance and a determined spirit that carried me through the decades.

I remember the cousins, the four boys and four girls. Among them was Shirley, a girl a little older than me, someone I considered a friend during those uncertain days when we didn't have a forever home. My heart still aches thinking of Joan, one of my older cousins, who had already known the bitterness of marriage and its scars. She had a little boy, Danny, who was born an albino. His white hair resembled strands of dried straw, his pink eyes filled with a quiet curiosity. Danny lived with his mother, Joan, after she divorced her husband, a decision made after discovering he had an STD (sexually transmitted disease). She blamed the STD for Danny's condition. This open secret cast a shadow over this innocent boy.

I remember the first time I saw Danny. His presence was like a ghost. He was a fragile, striking figure who somehow commanded attention without trying. The other children's eyes would initially be filled with curiosity, then quickly twist into smirks of ridicule. Danny's eyes, forever darting around, never still, seemed to give away his vulnerability. The kids, including my boy cousins, were merciless. Their teasing was cruel and relentless, aimed at his difference, their cruelty born of their own ignorance and fear.

They also teased me while encouraging me to join in mocking Danny, and I sometimes found myself caught between empathy and the desire to fit in. Danny looked miserable.

In those days, I didn't understand the pain that bullying caused or the loneliness in Danny. I was just a child, helpless and naive.

As I remember those days, I realize how much I longed to protect Danny, to see beyond his pale skin and darting eyes, to know who he really was. All those childhood wounds I witnessed, the cruelty and the misunderstandings, taught me the importance of empathy. True kindness often begins with understanding those who are different from us, even when we are young and unwise. My childhood was scarred with pain, yet it gave me a deeper sense of empathy that grew stronger with time. I have also come to learn that behind every act of cruelty is a cry for understanding, and possibly, a reflection of one's own pain and closed heart.

Aunty Rose and uncle Charlie did not have an Anderson shelter in the garden, but they had a Morrison shelter in the living room. This was a huge iron table structure with mesh sides and iron legs. It was solid as a rock. The floor area under the table was used as a sleeping space when there were no air raids. When the siren went off, we would huddle under the table or, sometimes, in one of the coat closets. It replaced the usual dining room table, and we ate meals at the Morrison shelter table.

My mother was happy to be near her own mother and sister again. Yet, we could all sense uncle Charlie's negative, toxic energy. He didn't want us there, and there were tense silences and lingering glances that I, as a child, could not understand but absorbed deeply. Their dislike of each other seemed to cut through our small and loving family, and I learned from their dynamic that some wounds are invisible and some conflicts are rooted deep.

Three of my girl cousins, all teenagers, became role models to me. I loved watching them put on make-up and get ready to go out, a universal mating ritual to attract the opposite gender, steeped in normalcy and defiance despite the bleakness of war. Joan, the eldest, often wore a striking black dress with delicate mesh sleeves, a rare sight in those austere days.

We didn't have many opportunities to go anywhere, but occasionally, we'd attend some function at the Village Hall. Those evenings suddenly pulsed with possibility and excitement. We'd pull heavy blackout curtains over every window, trying desperately to block out the light that might reveal us to unseen enemies flying above. It was a small act of rebellion in strange, unsettling times of war.

Officially, we were no longer evacuees as we lived with family, but we were still treated as if we were in exile at school. My friendship with my cousin Shirley, a girl about my age, offered moments of tentative stability, and we enjoyed spending time together.

My mother, in her relentless pursuit to provide for her children and give us greater security, took on more menial jobs wherever she could find them. With each modest paycheck, she somehow managed to buy me the tap dancing shoes I longed for. They were bright red, second-hand, but precious to me nonetheless. I was eager to learn, and each step I tapped helped me focus on the joy of dancing.

After every lesson, I would perform the routines at the temporary place where we lived, parading in front of the family and singing songs from my heart. Those nightly talent shows instilled a love of singing and dancing that has carried me through decades of joys and sorrows.

This shared love of music and performance created a bond that kept us going as a family through difficult times. Dame Vera Lynn was a cherished singer of this era, her voice resonating through radios as she sang songs about hopes for a brighter future. I remember listening intently, singing along quietly. I still remember the stirring melody of "When they sound the last all clear" and the haunting beauty of "The White Cliffs of Dover," as well as "We'll Meet Again" and "A Nightingale Sang in Berkeley Square."

Those songs, simple yet profound, gave us a spark of optimism, a fleeting belief that peace would someday return after the long, intense years of hardship. Our family had this ritual, and everyone was expected to perform in our small makeshift concerts; music somehow brought us closer. Aunty Rose and uncle Charlie owned a piano. It was an old relic and out of tune, yet magically came alive under mum's gentle and talented touch during these evening concerts, especially when there was no piercing air raid. Her piano playing was ethereal and filled our modest home with warmth, and lifted and soothed our weary, battered spirits. My brothers Ian and Alan, both gifted with a natural talent for the harmonica, would often entertain us with their breathy melodies, their faces twisting with concentration and pride.

I had to sleep on a worn-out couch in the same small room as Granny, who was frail and bent with rheumatoid arthritis. Her bedroom was a small, ground-floor space, always bustling with family members. She was constantly smoking, talking loudly, and laughing until she drifted into sleep. It was a struggle to find silence and rest, with the constant presence of visitors. Granny liked a light left on all night. I was different; I longed for complete darkness, for silence and solitude. Staying awake until the visitors left meant I had to hide under my covers, my nose pressed against the cold fabric, trying to block out the smoke and noise.

Sometimes I slipped under the Morrison shelter, the metal cage that offered a fragile sanctuary, but even there, the permeating smell of cigarette smoke was unavoidable and unbearable. Back then, we didn't know that smoking, and even second-hand smoke, was harmful. No one knew about cancer back then, and smoking was a social custom that many children like me grew up wanting to imitate.

When Frank, the oldest of the cousins, joined the Navy, the quiet in the house deepened; one less person to fill the space and the noise. But his absence was surprisingly felt sharply, a sad reminder of the ongoing sacrifices of war.

My cousin Peter, who was around my brother Ian's age, was close with my brothers. He became the leader of our adventures. Together, we explored the outskirts of our world and sometimes wandered around a nearby quarry. It was forbidden territory, with steep, sandy sides that beckoned us on warm, lazy days. We knew we shouldn't go there, but curiosity and the thrill of rebellion pulled us in. The boys slid down the slopes, splashing into the cold, murky water below, our laughter mingling with the shouting.

I never learned to swim because I was always afraid of the water. My brothers couldn't swim either, but somehow, our cousins would leap off the top, daringly while shouting. They were utterly fearless. Watching from a distance, my cousin Shirley and I would cling to each other, hearts pounding, afraid to join yet unable to look away. Despite the danger, my brothers never gave up trying and clambered up the slopes with scraped knees and muddy hands, brave in their own uncertain way.

As the new school term began that September after summer, I faced a fresh wave of anxiety. My new classroom felt cavernous and cold, and I hated it immediately. I ran all the way home at recess to find my mother. But she was firm; I was told I had to go back.

From that point on, I began to suffer from bullying, and it didn't stop for most of my school years. Some local girls picked on me because I was an evacuee, an outsider in the village. That feeling of being different, of not belonging, haunted me then and for years afterwards. Poverty compounded my sense of isolation. Our dinners at school were free, a small mercy that only branded me further as a strange outsider to pick on in the eyes of some children. The shame of being singled out was another layer of hurt, and I quietly bore that shame.

My 14-year-old cousin John, older and rougher, liked to pick on me too. The bullying was relentless, at school and at home. I was shy and awkward, afraid to fight back, which only made me an even easier target. I had learned early that while cruelty can come from the most unexpected sources and even from teachers, sometimes, silence is the only and best defence. The traumatic memories and scars from that time, both emotional and physical, still linger with me, which proves that time does not heal all wounds.

Sadly, bullies are everywhere, and their methods are universal and remain the same. It is now cloaked in more subtle forms; sometimes crueller, more insidious, creeping into everyday life and the workforce. Back then, I desperately sought a sanctuary where I could be alone with my thoughts and find some peace in a busy house where I learned to avoid mean cousins. Books became my escape, giving me imaginary worlds to escape to in the quiet of the Morrison shelter or in my secret corners. I'd crawl into that dark, cramped space, clutching my comics or a book, the muffled sounds of the house fading away.

My blankets, draped like curtains around me, created a tiny, cozy refuge. There, Hurricane, our loyal cat, would curl beside me, his fur a warm, steady presence offering comfort. Spitfire, the lively warplane-named cat owned by my cousins, would often hop onto my lap, purring softly, giving me small moments of joy. In those precious moments, I found a brief respite from war, poverty and painful bullying.

Another simple joy of my childhood was visiting the local fish and chip shop and paying a penny for battered scraps of fish. Munching on those greasy, crispy morsels on our walk home felt like the greatest treat. Those bites, so simple yet so satisfying, are a wonderful memory and a lasting lesson in finding happiness in the little things.

But life was changing. Granny's health declined, and she suffered greatly from rheumatoid arthritis. The pain etched lines into her face that I couldn't fully understand then, but I sensed the heaviness of her suffering. One day, my aunty Rose told us that Granny had to go to a hospital for old people at St. Albright's hospital. The thought of her being taken away was frightening, yet I didn't have the words to explain why.

We made the journey to visit her regularly by taking a bus from Colchester to Stanway, a suburb that felt foreign and distant. We spent a couple of hours in her sterile room, where she had some boiled sweets in a crumpled paper bag. Once hard and shiny, now the candies had softened over time, their surface mottled with fluff, hairs, and dust. I remember the repulsion I felt when the bag was opened, instinctively recoiling at the sight of those fuzzy, unclean sweets. Granny's eyes, clouded by cataracts, couldn't see the dirt, but to my young eyes, it was obvious. I would take a sweet out of politeness, knowing my brother Alan and I would look at each other with disgust and see who would dare to be brave enough to put the dirty, sticky sweet in their mouth first.

In those visits, I learned about the often harsh reality of ageing and illness. When we whined about the dirty sweets, mum's pragmatic voice cut through my innocent hesitation, "You've got to eat a speck of dirt before you die." Her words, direct and practical and unsympathetic, stayed with me. They taught me that life's hardships are unavoidable, but the way we face them shapes how we respond, which can help us overcome them. Looking back now, I see those childhood wounds – those feelings of fear, discomfort, and helplessness – were the roots of my strength, the scars that helped me understand what it means to be resilient.

CHAPTER 8

Bee Stings and Doll Clothes

My cousins, brothers, and I would spend countless hours wandering through the village, our footsteps tracing familiar paths as we explored the woods that surrounded us like an endless, mysterious kingdom. Those days felt like beautiful moments of pure magic. Building a hideout in the sturdy branches of a towering tree, or clearing a small patch in the thick undergrowth to carve out our secret world.

I remember how the woods would sometimes be alive with the delicate shimmer of bluebells and primroses, their sweet scent drifting softly through the air. We would gather handfuls of these fragile blue, pink and red flowers, and planned to take them home to show our mothers.

But how often we were disappointed when the flowers would wither and die soon after, their brief beauty and magic slipping away, a disturbing lesson in the fragility of nature. Bluebells, I learned, did not like to be harvested. Their sadness was written in the way their stems drooped. The primroses, a little sturdier, would sometimes survive a few days in water in a jam jar at aunty Rose and uncle Charlie's home, teaching me that even in death, there is a glimmer of life.

I never liked climbing trees. The bugs and spiders that crawled and skittered among the branches filled me with fear. Those tiny, relentless creatures seemed like monsters to me. I had nightmares about them crawling into my hair. My hair was long back then, white-blonde and flowing down to my waist, a tangled mess that I desperately feared would become a nest for creepy crawlies. So, I stayed safely on the ground while the boys dared the heights, their laughter drifting down from above.

One hot summer day, Alan, my brave older brother, decided to climb a tall, sturdy tree. I watched anxiously from below, my stomach twisting as he disappeared into the leafy canopy. Suddenly, he came tumbling down, screaming in terror. A swarm of wasps was buzzing viciously around his head and shoulders. Alan was badly stung in his nose! We all lurched in panic and ran as fast as we could back home. Tears streaming down Alan's face, his cries echoing through the woods.

When we reached the safety of home, mum didn't hesitate. She hurried him to the doctor's, where he was treated for multiple stings, some swollen painfully, but thankfully with no lasting damage. That day, my eyes were opened to the dangers lurking in the woods, and I learned to exercise caution and respect for nature. Alan was more careful after that, his childhood bravado tempered by pain.

In another quiet, lonely moment, I wandered into the woods and happened upon a strange sight: scattered dolls' clothes tossed among the leaves and tangled branches. I gathered them carefully and carried them home, feeling a sense of wonder and curiosity. I showed my mother, puzzled by their presence. We couldn't understand why they had been abandoned there. No doll accompanied them, nothing to tell a story of joy or sadness. I, who had never owned a doll of my own, played with those discarded clothes as if they were the costumes of a cherished friend, dressing an imaginary doll, imagining stories that never truly belonged to me.

Later that day, a knock at the door broke the quiet. It was the mother of the twins, a pair of girls who had been vicious to me at school. Without greeting, she accused me, her voice cold and accusing, "Your daughter stole my girl's doll clothes."

My mother stood firm, defending me. "No," she said gently, "they were thrown away in the woods, and Joy simply picked them up."

The woman's eyes narrowed. "They belong to us. I want them back."

My mother's voice was calm but firm. "Give them to her, Joy," she said softly. "I know you didn't steal them. Maybe the girls will take better care of them now."

I hesitated but handed over the tiny, ragged clothes, feeling the sting of injustice and shame. I hated those twins. I knew they would tease me even more at school. I knew they had dolls and a pram for them, and I wondered if the clothes belonged to them, but I said nothing because they bullied me mercilessly at school.

I wondered how their mother knew to come to our door, if they had been watching, waiting perhaps to see who would take the fallen clothes.

I never had a doll growing up. Those plastic or porcelain figures seemed like distant, unattainable treasures. But later in life, my daughter bought me a doll, a symbol of something I had missed. When my daughters were young, my mother and I spent many hours knitting tiny doll clothes for them out of love. And though I no longer long for dolls or childish pleasures, I knitted many dolls and toys for my children, grandchildren, and others – over the years, pieces of my love were woven into yarn and fabric. Now, looking back on my deprived childhood through the lens of nearly a century, I'm grateful it wasn't lacking in a mother's love. Her unconditional support provided me with the quiet strength to overcome deprivation.

CHAPTER 9

Blackberries and bombs

August 17, 1943 was a day engraved into my memory forever. It was mum's forty-fourth birthday, a day that would suddenly and forever alter the lives within our modest house on Heath Road where we lived with aunty Rose's family. Behind our home sprawled a stretch of land we called 'the Governments,' a zone used by soldiers for military drills, target practice, and mock battles. When they trained, a bright red flag fluttered, warning us to keep away.

Entering this zone was strictly forbidden, yet for us children, it was also a tantalizing playground filled with the plumpest, juiciest blackberries we had ever tasted. The scent of ripe berries was intoxicating and tempting enough to make us climb the fence that separated our garden from that forbidden territory.

On that particular day, Ian, Alan, and our cousin Peter decided to venture into the field to gather blackberries. The red flag was no longer flying, and the area appeared deserted. We often heard the distant crackle of rifle fire and the thunderous explosions during nearby army drills. Our back garden looked out onto the thicket of bushes and the fence that separated our home from what felt like forbidden territory.

Carefully, they climbed over the fence, each carrying a container for the berries and a sack that Alan had brought along. I stood watching from the yard, eager to join them, but they made it clear I was not welcome. Their words were sharp and dismissive, telling me to "Buzz off" and not bother them.

After breakfast, they set out, their basket and sack in hand, leaving me behind. I never thought to ask what the sack was for. They were gone for what felt like hours, returning just as we sat down for lunch.

I had waited on the back steps until mum called me in for lunch, my eyes flicking back and forth from the fence to the house, my stomach aching to know what they had brought back and wanting to taste the little blackberries.

When they returned, they came through the hedge, Ian leading the way with a determined look, followed by Alan, who was carrying a heavy sack slung over his shoulder. I could see from where I stood that whatever was inside the sack was not blackberries, and an uneasy feeling settled in my gut.

Peter came last, carrying a small basket with a few blackberries in it. Alan, looking pale and tired, dumped the sack onto the ground and limped into the house. He had a stitch in his side from carrying the heavy load. Inside, mum quickly put him to bed to rest until the pain subsided – it seemed like an ominous sign of what was yet to come.

Peter and Ian wandered down the winding path of the garden and hurried into the house with an air of secrecy.

I asked softly, "What have you got?"

Ian's voice was defensive and sharp as he snapped back, "Nothing. Stay away, you're just a girl, so mind your own business."

I remember the way mum called them into the kitchen, her voice gentle but firm, and we all sat down for a simple lunch that somehow felt like a fragile peace. The two boys ate quickly, their hands trembling slightly as they devoured fried cheese and onions on toast, and then they hurried into the garden once more.

I was upset, and felt a mix of frustration and helplessness, because they wouldn't let me share in whatever secret they were hiding. I blurted out before I could stop myself, "They have some secret stuff in the sack and they got them over at the Government's!"

My mother and aunty Rose exchanged a glance that spoke volumes, their eyes narrowing in shared concern, and both got up from the table simultaneously. I rose too, feeling the weight of my words hanging in the air, and uncle Charlie followed us out through the kitchen door.

Just as we stepped outside, an incredible explosion shattered the peacefulness of the afternoon. The house trembled as if the very bones of the earth had been shaken, windows rattling violently as smoke billowed in swirling, chaotic patterns around us. We all screamed, instinctively ducking and shielding our faces. Our eyes darted nervously toward the direction of the blast, the garden where the explosion erupted.

I could see Ian kneeling, bleeding and screaming. His body was pierced in many places, blood pouring out of several holes that looked like small fountains spurting. His clothes had been ripped from his body.

There was no sign of Peter at all, only disarray and chaos spreading through the yard like wildfire. I could still hear mum's tired moans of "Oh Ian," a heartbreaking sound that I can hear clearly even today, many decades later. I wondered where Peter had gone; his absence filled my heart with panic.

Aunty Rose ran up the garden path with frantic urgency, her face streaked with tears, closely followed by uncle Charlie, both screaming. The noise was almost too much to bear, a haunting grief. Then aunty Rose suddenly started moaning as if she were a trapped animal, her voice rising in desperate keening that sounded utterly raw and unfiltered. Without warning, she turned and ran back down the garden, making sounds I had never heard before. It was an awful, piercing crying that seemed to come from some deep, primal place within her. She had seen a body part of her son Peter and knew innately that he had been blown to pieces.

My mother was crying, her grief cut my heart. Neighbours rushed in, alarms sounded, and an ambulance arrived. Ian was hurried away to the hospital, already bleeding and covered with shrapnel. For weeks, he lay in a hospital bed, doctors painstakingly removing fragments from his body and some landed perilously close to his heart. Miraculously, he survived. He was lucky to be alive.

Peter, who had picked up the object they had found and slammed it against the ground, took the full force of the explosion. Pieces of his body were strewn around the garden and in the bushes. His body parts were collected in a wheelbarrow and taken away.

Alan was fortunate to survive, too, because he had managed to carry the strange object back in the sack on his back, and with trembling hands, he dumped it down with a thud. I often think about that moment now, after all these years, and wonder how he must have felt.

Aunty Rose and uncle Charlie were extremely distraught, their pain, shock and grief heavy and palpable that seeped into every corner of the house. Ian had somehow escaped death, while Peter's life had been stolen in an instant – this didn't seem fair and it was something we all thought but never said out loud.

The house was divided, fractured by a profound pain that none of us knew how to contain or process. All our cousins sat in silence, their faces etched with grief for their brother. They had no words for us, just quiet mourning. I remember how fragile life seemed then, how shocking it was to realize that a life could be taken so quickly.

My brother Alan, just a boy of nine, was asked to be a witness and describe the object that had exploded to the Coroner. They wondered if he could draw it, as if a picture could somehow dispel the confusion better than words. And he succeeded. He was a good artist.

It turned out that what they'd found was an unexploded Mills Bomb, a sinister relic that somehow had come into their hands. The Coroner praised Alan for his skill, for capturing the contents of that sack with such accuracy. I recall feeling a strange mix of pride and fear, knowing how young he was. The official verdict was that it was an accidental death, yet nothing could truly explain the traumatic ache that lingered in our hearts.

The house felt colder and more distant after that day, as though a deep freeze had settled over us. Nobody knew the right words to say or the right things to do; all we could do was endure. It was an incredibly tragic time, and as I look back now after many decades, I see how life's fragility can teach us the importance of holding on to each other amid senseless tragedy.

Mum and her sister, Rose, loved each other deeply, yet mum understood that it was time to leave and to continue her life with her children on her own. Aunty Rose and uncle Charlie now needed space to mourn and to organize their son's funeral, a task that seemed overwhelming yet necessary. Ian was confined to a hospital in Colchester, so now we had two people to visit – Ian and Granny. Colin was still serving with the Fleet Air Arm, which meant mum, Alan, and I would eventually move on to another place and deal with uncertainty again.

Soon after, mum revealed she had found a small, humble cottage in Wivenhoe, just across the River Colne from Rowhedge. The rent was astonishing and was only one shilling a week. It was an almost unbelievable bargain.

We packed our single trunk once more. It was the same one we had in the shelter in Ashford, and we carefully made our way down to the ferry across the river to our new home in Wivenhoe. The house was in a deplorable state, deemed unfit for living and marked for demolition, but, as the war still raged, we somehow managed to rent it. I never knew how mum discovered this fragile refuge, but from 1943 until 1958, it became our long-term home.

We lived there until we eventually emigrated to Canada, leaving behind Colin, who stayed in England after leaving the Fleet Air Arm. The entire row of houses was eventually torn down to make way for new townhomes, but at the time, that little place in Wivenhoe felt like a miracle.

That dreadful day on August 17, 1943, which happened to be my mother's forty-fourth birthday, influenced much of who I am today. It was a moment of such intense trauma that I have carried it with me through every passing year. Even now, in 2025, I can still see it with startling clarity, as if it occurred only yesterday rather than more than eighty years ago.

Life taught me early that suffering often comes without warning, revealing the strange and sometimes frightening ways childhood experiences shape us over time. But I've found that processing the sorrow can give us an unshakable strength to face many more storms. I wanted to share these memories – the good, bad, and ugly – with my children, grandchildren, and friends. These moments are all the more precious because, though tinged with joy, hope, and pain, they are filled with the quiet, gentle resolve to take one day at a time that comes from survival.

Part II: Coming of Age
1943 – 1958

ACROSS THE RIVER IN WIVENHOE

CHAPTER 10

The Crossing

The River Colne was truly the beating heart of all those small villages that lined its shores. It wasn't just a body of water; it felt alive, full of stories and sounds that seemed to resonate and get passed down from one generation to the next. The village of Rowhedge, which we were just leaving behind, was a hive of activity – houses, shops, and pubs all crowded tightly along the quayside. Boats were moored just a few feet from the edge, bobbing gently in the water, some tied to the posts, others drifting lazily with the current.

Looking out over the river, it was clear that life revolved around it. You could hear the constant hum of boats sounding horns, fishermen shouting out, calling in their catches as the dark waters shimmered and rippled under the sun. People strolled along, watching the boats and talking in quiet and sometimes loud voices, their footsteps in staccato step with the distant call of seagulls and the occasional splash of a paddle.

This was the Rowhedge side of the river. We were waiting there that day for a small, manual ferry to carry us across to Wivenhoe, which was also in Essex and just a few miles away.

The River Colne made its way northward, eventually pouring into the immense North Sea. When I first looked at it, years ago, all I saw was a muddy, smelly, black expanse of water. It was dirty and uninviting, and I remember wondering how anyone could cross it without getting lost or worse.

The ferry was just a tiny wooden rowboat, no bigger than a large bathtub, with a couple of oars and an old, weathered look that made it seem almost fragile. I held my breath, wondering if we could all squeeze into it with all our belongings, to fit beneath the worn wooden sides. I hoped the boat wouldn't sink under the weight of us.

When the ferry boat finally reached the quay, the ferryman was a rough-looking man, cigarette dangling from his lips, a filthy old cap pushed down on his head. He grabbed hold of the boat, steadying it in the water while we climbed in, dragging our bags and possessions along. Everything we owned was with us, packed into whatever we could carry, and it suddenly felt incredibly important not to leave anything behind. We all had to squeeze onto one small seat, sitting very close, shoulder to shoulder, which was quite uncomfortable.

I was afraid of the river then. Afraid of the muddy darkness that seemed endless and full of unknown dangers. I remember wishing we didn't have to cross, wishing I could stay on the safe side where things made more sense. Yet I also knew that a new life was waiting somewhere over that water. I clung to the hope that this change might bring better days, that somehow moving from all eight different places we had lived in over those difficult years could be a step toward something better.

Back then, I had no inkling that I was about to almost drown in that muddy river, and that I would be rescued. I recall daring to walk across at low tide, my feet squishing in the thick mud beneath me, fear rising in my chest as I hoped the tide would hold until we could return. But it didn't, and in the end, we paid the ferryman to take us home.

From this crossing, I learned that fear is often just a feeling we can face, even when we don't feel brave enough. The river was a barrier then, but it also became a parable of how I learned to keep going no matter how muddy or uncertain the path seemed. Crossing that water was a small act of courage, one that motivated me to take on bigger fears.

When we finally reached the other side, Wivenhoe's quayside wasn't directly opposite Rowhedge's quayside but was instead set a couple of miles further along the river's bend. It was situated right in the middle of the village, a little further away from the mouth of the river. The Wivenhoe quayside was opposite the village of Fingringhoe. There was another ferry that would take people back and forth along the river, crossing at different points; yet another reminder of how life on the water was always about transfer, transition, and movement.

After crossing the river, we had about two miles to walk before reaching the house, and it felt like the longest walk in the world to me. There was a narrow, winding path that stretched out in front of us for several metres, just a faint strip of dirt amid overgrown grass. Then came the style, a simple wooden structure, but to a girl like me, it looked tall and imposing. We had to climb over it, and I remember how my mother hesitated, her face full of concern, eyes fixed on the other side.

Beyond the style was a field, and in that field, a herd of cows. Even now, I can still see their big, curious eyes watching us, their massive bodies silent and unmoving. My mother was terrified of cows. She had been chased by a bull when she was a girl and her childhood was haunted by that fear. That fright also stayed with her all her life, and it included any bovine creature that looked like a bull – anything big, heavy, and unpredictable. She refused point-blank to step into the field. No reasoning could sway her. But we didn't have much choice that day.

Both Alan and I grabbed her arms firmly and dragged her across the field. She was sandwiched between us and clung to us while the cows just stared at us. We moved slowly, heads bowed down, trying not to make eye contact with the cows. I knew enough to understand that animals could sense fear. I kept my eyes on the ground, counting my steps, wishing I could make everything disappear. Thankfully, these cows did not chase us. When we finally reached the next style, my mother sighed with relief and hurried through, glad to leave the cows behind. Just as I learned from the ferry crossing, sometimes you just have to push through the fear, even when your heart is pounding with terror.

After we managed to calm our mother down, Alan and I went back across the field, retrieved the trunk and carried it carefully to the other side. Walking along, I kept thinking how different life was, so full of small obstacles that felt like mountains.

From there, our walk took us past a lumber yard, with piles of rough timber stacked high and the noise of saws. We passed the Station pub near the Railway Station, a place crowded with folks coming and going, full of the kind of life I didn't fully understand at the time. The road stretched out before us, leading toward the quayside. We saw a Community Hall there too, and many boats and houses.

That place, the quayside, was more than just a landing spot for boats. It was a gathering place where people came together to share stories, to celebrate, to forget their worries for a while. I remember attending many of those events in the years to come: regattas where boats raced like wild horses across the water, dances on homemade platforms that wobbled but brought everyone joy, and Beauty contests. When the war was over, those gatherings transformed into many spontaneous parties and celebrations filled with laughter and relief.

On that particular day of 1943, I did not know all this history, all these stories. I only knew that I wanted to get away from the river, from the fears and uncertainties of war, and see the house where we would try to start anew. We walked up Anchor Hill to the High Street, a place full of memories even then. Opposite the old church of St. Mary the Virgin, we found Blythe's Lane. I remember how it looked then, just a narrow, dusty path winding through the houses. It used to be called Blood Alley because right at the bottom of that lane was a slaughterhouse, a place full of bloodshed. Even the names of places held stories of hardship, of survival, of learning to live with fears and scars. Life then was a lesson in persevering through all obstacles, and I carried that lesson with me all my days.

Joy's painting of St. Mary's Church in Wivenhoe,
which she completed in 2015.

Blood Alley

We made our way slowly down the narrow laneway to No. 4
Blythe's Lane in the village of Wivenhoe. That house was going
to be our home for what felt like forever at the time, a coming-
of-age place where I would explore more of life in all its rough,
unpolished beauty and pain. Opposite Blythe's Lane, which
most locals still called Blood Alley, was the church of St. Mary
the Virgin and a small pub called The Falcon. Not far up the
street was the Grosvenor Pub, sitting a little north on the busy
stretch of the High Street.

Our house was part of a row of seven terraced homes, each
with two rooms on the ground and two above. The front of
each house had a long, narrow garden, and at the very end,
there was a little wooden outhouse. The outhouse shared a
wall with the neighbour's, a reminder of how closely bound
our lives were in those days. The first four houses in the row

shared a single water tap in the backyard, and the last three shared another. Not one of those houses had running water inside, a fact you didn't realize until you had to fetch water day after day.

Each house had a humble wooden lean-to shed in the backyard, directly opposite the back door. That's where we stored coal and kept a tub for hand laundry, which we did outside, no matter the weather. The houses had been condemned long ago as unfit for living, but people still squeezed in, as if somehow that made it right. Number 4 was the only one vacant, and I never knew who mum paid the rent to; maybe the landlord or a distant figure we never saw; she always paid on time.

Stepping inside the house made us feel dismayed. Peeling wallpaper clung to damp walls, and patches of mould and discoloured paint told silent stories of neglect. There was a fireplace in the front room, sitting cold and unused, and a gas ring with a metre on the floor just inside the door. The back room had a wood or coal stove, a cupboard underneath the stairs, and a tall cupboard reaching up to the ceiling. Mice scurried around constantly, darting behind furniture and along the walls; their presence was unsettling. Large harvest spiders hung silently from the ceiling, their legs like dark brushes touching the air. Outside, the long garden stretched out, overgrown and untended, with a worn path beaten down by countless footsteps to the outhouse. That garden was badly neglected and reflected its own stories of hardship.

We had to carry water into the house for washing and cooking, filling a bucket from the shared tap outside. That routine was a daily reminder of all we lacked. The gas ring on the floor was attached to the gas metre, and it required shillings to turn on. Mum would kneel on the dusty floor to cook or make tea, always careful, always patient. Old furniture was left behind, probably because the previous tenant had died or moved away, leaving pieces that had seen better days.

Upstairs was reached by a set of wooden stairs near the back door. In the two small rooms upstairs, mattresses lay directly on the floor, thin and battered, but they served as beds nonetheless. The front room had an old dressing table and a chest of drawers that managed to hold all of our small belongings. Each bedroom had a tiny closet with hooks for clothes. Alan would have his own room, and mum and I would share the other one. When Ian came home from the hospital, he and Alan would share a room. That room was infested with bed bugs, creatures that had made their home in the faded wallpaper and they were full of blood, as I would later learn.

Every room had cockroaches, many of them, hiding during the day, creeping out at night. The mice saw our house as their home, and I learned early on how to catch them and take them outside gently, never wanting to kill. Life in those walls was brutally difficult, and I think about it often now, as I try to understand how we survived those tough years. I believe it was love and hope that carried us through.

Despite the initial feelings of despair and disappointment, I ended up living there for fifteen long years of my young life. It was not by choice – truly, no alternative existed. My mother was a single woman trying to raise three children at a time, which was neither kind nor forgiving to women without husbands. Back then, single mothers were not eligible for government housing, like a council home. Even as we all grew older and started working, contributing whatever we could, there was no way out of that difficult housing dilemma we found ourselves in.

I suppose there was a small comfort in finally having a place to call our own. After years of moving from one spare room to another in other people's homes, living like unwanted guests, we had crossed a threshold from being homeless evacuees to being ordinary people with a rented space of our own. We made what we could of it, trying to clean and tidy it up, and inject a little bit of cheer into the worn-out walls, because there is always a spark of something hopeful in simply making a space for yourself.

It was far from a palace, of course. Wivenhoe was on the opposite side of the river from Rowhedge where we lived with aunty Rose and uncle Charlie. That meant nobody knew us here, and, strangely, it felt like a kind of relief. We were strangers, and in some twisted way, that meant we could start again. As a child, I felt shame about our history, of the hardships we'd endured. Moving forward meant leaving that shame behind, or so I believed at the time.

Yet some things never change, and I learned that lesson very quickly. Village memories are long and deep. People here still called our new home Blood Alley, even though the slaughterhouse had long been shut down and the name had been changed officially. Our house, along with the others nearby, had long been under the threat of demolition plans. But as long as there were families like ours desperate enough to live in those dilapidated places, those houses remained leased, kept alive by hope or necessity.

These houses were sturdy, made of brick with a kind of stubbornness about them. Between houses two and three, there was a narrow passageway, and another between five and six leading to the backyard. All of this was just concrete, rough and unpolished, with a small wooden shed for each home tucked away. Our water came from a tap situated between those two houses, an old-fashioned faucet that sputtered and groaned when turned on. Filling a bucket was a slow, careful task, balancing the weight and trying not to spill. We carried the water into the house for everyday chores, for cooking and washing.

Hot water was a luxury, heated over the gas ring on the stovetop, which required a certain skill from my mother to manage. Balancing that heavy bucket on the gas stove was a tricky dance, one she had to master with patience and concentration.

My selfless mother was determined to give us a better life. When she found a job, she saved every penny she could for a proper stove. It wasn't easy, but she scraped together enough for a deposit and went to Curry's to place an order for an electric stove. When it arrived, I remember it felt like Christmas morning. It was a symbol of progress and efficiency. Now mum could stand to cook instead of kneeling, as her back ached from the constant strain.

She also took care of the laundry in that old wooden shed outside. Heating water was a slow process. Once it was ready, she used a scrubbing board and a brush to wash our clothes, each piece was scrubbed thoroughly, then passed through a mangle to squeeze out excess water. It was hard, physical work, but she did it without complaint. Afterwards, everything was hung out on a line in the front yard, fluttering in the wind like makeshift banners of hope. If the weather turned rainy, the clothes would be brought inside, draped over any available surface, waiting for the sun or her careful eye to decide when they were dry enough to wear or iron.

I see how these small acts and everyday struggles moulded us. Hope is found in the quiet, persistent effort to make life better, step by tiny step.

There were keys to both the front and back doors, but they were never locked. It was a strange, carefree feeling to know that the possessions inside had little to no value, at least in the eyes of the world. The front door had no letterbox, so the postman would open the door, shout "Post" and toss the mail inside without ever setting foot over the threshold. We never really understood the importance of guarding things or privacy – that was just how it was.

The toilet in the shed at the top of the front garden was a little piece of hardship in our daily lives. It had a pull chain and a cracked wooden seat that looked ready to break. We had to use tiny squares of newspaper to wipe ourselves, threaded onto a piece of string like some primitive toilet paper bouquet. We learned to be careful with how many squares we tore off because if we used too many, the toilet would clog. It was a constant balancing act.

During the cold winter months, the tank of that outside toilet would freeze solid. We would have to carry boiling water from the house, carefully pouring it into the tank to thaw out the ice inside. I remember waiting anxiously, shivering, while the water slowly melted away the frost. Most often, I would hold my bowels until I arrived at school to use the toilet. The school toilets had a shiny, smooth kind of paper that was barely absorbent but felt a little more like comfort.

I hated being in the loo when the neighbour was on his toilet on the other side of the flimsy partition. The old wooden barrier was full of holes, and privacy was a joke. It was as if the whole world – or at least that tiny slice of my world – was open and exposed. The toilet at home was also home to many big spiders, harvest spiders we called them. I lived in constant dread that one would drop on me at any moment. When I saw them in the house, I would scream and run, my heart pounding.

Joy, aged 8, and her brother, Alan, aged 9, and their half of the outhouse in the background.

The toilets at school were always clean and fairly private, and always functioning properly. One day, I began my long habit of holding my bowel movements until I got to school, just to avoid the awkwardness. That habit, of course, made me very constipated.

The couple who lived at house number 5 were elderly, and I remember how they seemed to spend all their time in the toilet. I would always rush out as soon as I could when someone else was in the neighbouring cubicle. It felt like an invasion of my privacy. I didn't know then about courteous behaviour or etiquette, and the courtesy flush of the toilet. I only learned about the concept of a courtesy flush much later, during an etiquette and protocol training class.

When we first moved into our home, it was filthy. Everything inside needed fixing, cleaning, and starting from scratch, sort of repair work. We all pitched in, despite not knowing how long we would stay. My mother held onto hopes of getting a council house, a fresh start somewhere else, but despite all our efforts, that hope never turned into reality.

CHAPTER 11

Starting School

We moved to the little village of Wivenhoe back in late August 1943. I remember my mother registering Alan and me for primary school, her hands gentle yet steady as she filled out the forms. She also managed to apply for a clothing grant to help with our school clothes and expenses, and because of our hardships at the time, she was granted that support. The money wasn't much, but it was enough to buy me a simple navy blue tunic and a white blouse, along with a pair of brown T-bar sandals from Marks and Spencer's. Alan's clothes were basic too – short grey trousers, a white shirt, and sandals that looked chunky but sturdy.

On our first morning at school, I felt a knot tighten in my stomach as we walked along High Street, crossing the railway bridge, and heading down that narrow lane beside the tracks to where the school was on Phillips Road. I was afraid to step into the school.

We had to go into the headmistress's office, which for a seven-year-old seemed like entering the lair of a beast. Miss Smith was her name. When we peered nervous at her from behind her desk, she looked up and boomed, "Oh, there you are, Joy and Alan Greenfield." Her voice was loud enough to make me jump. We both mumbled our responses, too shy to say much. I stared at Miss Smith and thought she looked like a man. She was tall with a face that felt plain and a bit rough, like she had seen too much. Her teeth were big and uneven, making me think of the wolf from the story of Red Riding Hood, which I'd read long before. Her nose was large and covered with red veins, and her hair partially covered her eyes, giving her a mysterious look.

Her haircut was a strange one; one side had a clump falling over her eyebrow, resembling something I'd later learn to associate with Hitler's hairstyle. The other side was cut short and was like a man's. I must have stared, honestly, because I had never seen anything like it before. She came out from behind her desk, dressed in a brown tweed suit that looked heavy and unimpressive.

"Come on," she said loudly, "Let's get you both to your classrooms." She strode down the corridor with big steps, and I scrambled to keep up. Alan was behind me, a few steps back.

Miss Smith's pleated skirt swung with each stride, making a soft swishing sound that seemed to echo in the quiet hallways. Her thick lyle cotton stockings made her legs look huge, and her clumpy shoes with thick heels sounded loud and firm as she marched us along. She left a mothball scent lingering in her wake, which reminded me of old closets.

Eventually, she pushed open a door and yelled out, "Here's the new girl, Joy Greenfield." Without waiting, she shoved me inside and turned away, leaving me standing at the front of a room full of curious children. I felt small and exposed, my heart pounding in my chest. Alan had followed Miss Smith to his classroom, which was filled with children about his age.

"There's a seat over there," the teacher said to me, pointing with her finger. I made my way over and sat down quietly, feeling self-conscious. As I looked around that classroom, I began to realize that Miss Smith was not quite the monster I'd first thought. Yes, she ruled with an iron fist, caned naughty children, and her glare could make a child's spine stiffen. But I learned she was fair, and later, I found out she was a lesbian whose partner was the deputy head of the school. That day, her fierce exterior frightened me, though.

Somewhere during that first day in that noisy, bustling classroom, someone handed me a small, folded note. I remember unfolding it carefully and reading the words, 'Dear Joy, I love you, do you love me? Love, Alan.' It was the first love note I ever received. The first time anyone had said they loved me. The boy's name was Alan Foster.

Then I took a piece of paper from the desk and wrote 'I love you too,' which I signed as Joy. When I passed it back, I felt a flutter in my stomach, overwhelmed by the strange but sweet feeling of being loved. I had a boyfriend! I kept his love note until the ink smudged and the paper disintegrated. It was my secret treasure.

A few days later, life threw another little challenge my way. We had dinner at school, a routine that I hated more than anything. Because our family was poor, dinner was free for both Alan and me. I hated the way the teachers announced it to the class. It just announced to everyone how poor we were. I burned with embarrassment, it was the same shame I'd felt at the previous school in Rowhedge.

On that particular day, during dinner, the server looked at me and said, "Hey, I hear you have a boyfriend." I was horrified. My cheeks burned hot, and I snapped, "Mind your own business." I felt terrible instantly, especially since my mother was also working. They both looked shocked.

I managed to whisper, while blushing so deeply, "I'm sorry." I thought I might disappear.

"I should think so," said my mother. I could tell she was angry with me, and I knew I would get a telling off when I got home. I did not argue with her. I also had to apologise properly to the server the next day and felt like I had let everyone down.

The following day, after lunch, feeling distinctly awful, I slipped away to the orchard on the school grounds, a peaceful corner. My boyfriend Alan was waiting for me there, and he gave me a rosy apple to help me feel better. The sweet, crisp fruit was a welcome reminder that even in times of distress, an act of kindness could lift my spirit.

Sometimes the boys and girls were separated in school, and I quickly learned about the girl gangs. Every new girl was bullied, and I was no exception. The leader of the girls' gang was a strong girl, and I was terrified of her. She pushed me against the wall once and demanded to know why I had no father. Rumours had spread that my mother was alone with four children.

She looked at me sharply and asked, "Where's your dad?" she asked.

"He's dead," I whispered, "he died in the war."

The truth, however, was far more complicated. I was too ashamed to tell her the truth that my father had left us just before the war started to be with another woman named Lily and that he had more children with her. I kept that secret locked inside, never sharing it with anyone. As a child, it was a heavy burden.

"When did he die?" demanded the girl.

"I don't know," I said, and I started to cry. She pushed me again, then she and the girls left me to pick on someone else. It was years before I could tell the truth about why we had no father at home. By then, I was aware of how badly he had treated my mother and felt there was no need to keep the secret.

The war was still raging on, casting a gloom over everything. One morning, not too long after I joined this new school, my teacher called my name in that steady, no-nonsense voice I knew so well.

"Stand up, Joy," she said. I jumped to my feet, unsure why I was being summoned, feeling a little nervous and curious at the same time.

Then she told me, "Your name has been changed, Joy. You are no longer Joy Greenfield. Now you are Joy MacRae."

I remember blushing, feeling the heat rush to my cheeks, and I mumbled, "Yes, miss."

"Sit down now, Joy," said the teacher.

As I sank into the chair, I remembered my mother mentioning that my father had legally changed our last name from Greenfield to MacRae. It was during a time when fear was at an all-time high over Hitler's threat to invade England, and some believed that our original name might be linked to

Jewish roots, which could be dangerous. Considering what was happening in Europe and how Hitler had already taken the Channel Islands, it made sense to change our name to protect ourselves.

That day at school, however, I felt like it was one more strike against me, another reason for questions I didn't have answers for. I just wanted to blend in and not attract the wrong kind of attention. It was a confusing time, and I learned early that sometimes, you had to just keep going and that survival often meant adaptation, even when it meant losing a piece of who you were.

Joy with her brother Alan and their mother in 1944.

Life at school

Each morning at school began with an assembly where all the children stood silently together. I remember feeling faint often, having to sit on the cold, hard floor just to catch my breath. My short tunic sometimes rode up as I sat, and I worried about my knickers showing. I had low blood pressure back then and still do now. Those fainting spells would sometimes come back, catching me off guard even after all these years.

Part of our school day was dedicated to exercise. We learned country dancing and folk songs, usually with a teacher who always sat sideways on the piano stool so she could keep an eye on us as we twirled and danced. She wore long knickers that reached her knees, which were quite fashionable at the time. I still remember how we used to laugh because her knickers were sometimes visible, and even at that young age, it made us giggle and feel a little mischievous.

I cherished those moments of singing and dancing at Wivenhoe Primary School. I did well at both, and they became something I loved deeply. I had been singing and dancing since I was four years old, starting in the early days of the war when we had to sing for our supper. Besides singing and dancing, I enjoyed sewing and knitting, and I was pretty good at those. I also loved English. Math was not my strength, but I managed to learn enough, which taught me that sometimes, persistence counts just as much as talent.

Recess was never my favourite part of the day. The school quickly learned I had been an evacuee and used that against me. My lack of a visible father and my changed name made me feel different, like an outsider. I wasn't the only girl bullied, but

I was definitely one of the most vulnerable. I never knew what went on in the boys' playground, but among the girls, a group of what we called the popular girls made life difficult for those of us who only wanted to belong.

One of the cruel rites of passage was a quick glance to check if your breasts were developing and a peek in your underwear to see if you had begun to grow pubic hair. I was only seven and there wasn't much to look at, but even then, those popular girls wanted to see how far along you were. Sometimes I wondered what it all meant or why it mattered so much to them.

Getting through the school day was rarely easy. There were small moments that brought some joy and comfort: free milk in small bottles each day, a splash of cod liver oil and orange juice handed out during breaks. I looked forward to those simple things, their familiarity offering some sense of routine.

One day, I sat down and wrote a composition about my cousin Peter's death. My mother was called to the school and told I had written a very morbid essay. She told the teacher it was because I had been there when he died and that I was just trying to tell the truth, to process, heal, and get it out of my system. (Thanks, mum, for your support!) Looking back now, I realize nobody really wanted to hear about a tragedy. We had enough of it during the war.

After that, I began focusing on happier, lighter subjects. After school, a bunch of boys and a group of girls would head over to the playing fields to play something called 'Kiss chase.' It was like hide and seek, but when you were caught, you had to kiss whoever found you. I always hoped Alan would be the one to find me, and mostly he was.

I liked Alan very much. I had a crush on him for years. Just before we left for Canada, I heard he was getting married to a girl from the village. I asked him why, and he just said, "Why do you think?" That was his way of saying it was all about sex, I suppose. Looking back, I feel I was too innocent and pure for my own good.

I ran into Alan again when I was sixty-five and celebrating in England. His birthday was a day before mine. I surprised him at his birthday party, and he said he had often thought about me over the years. We took a rare, great photo together, a reminder of those long lost days.

When I was nine, in 1945, I remember clearly the war finally ending. I remember the streets overflowing with celebration. There were street parties everywhere with long tables and chairs on either side set up right on the pavements, crowded with neighbours sharing what little they had. We raced around like silly goofs, eating jam tarts, cake, ice cream and drinking copious amounts of lemonade, grabbing a handful of broken biscuits courtesy of Woolworth's. It was a grand party.

Kids played games, and everyone smiled widely in relief and hope. It was a time to rejoice, knowing Hitler was defeated. We all danced to gramophones in the streets while music flowed through the air. Back then, traffic was rarely a problem. Cars were few and far between. The police had closed off the streets for these celebrations, making it easy for us kids to run around freely. The nearest party was in the lower High Street, close enough for us to walk to easily.

The streets looked bright and festive, decorated with homemade ornaments, draped all over the place. People were so happy because, for the first time in a long while, we felt safe. The war was over, and we could breathe again. As children, it felt like our first real taste of freedom and it meant a free party. We didn't care that the decorations were simple or that tables were covered with old sheets or newspapers. It wasn't elegant, but then, nothing was in those days. We recycled everything and threw nothing away, so whatever was available and suitable was used.

It was a joyous time for everyone, a respite from fear. No bombs falling, no hiding under tables, just the pure joy of being a child again. We finally felt unburdened and free. Hitler's end came by suicide in his underground bunker, a fitting end for a Nazi fascist and a man so cruel. I remember hearing Dame Vera Lynn's songs and believing that peace was finally coming. Her songs finally came true. The war, which had taken so many lives, was over.

Thank God and everyone who made that happen. There were so many lives lost, so many Allied soldiers with broken bodies returning home. What a relief that the Second World War was indeed over.

CHAPTER 12

Village Life in Blood Alley

When we first arrived in the small, quiet village of Wivenhoe, I was just a girl trying to find my footing. It was me, my mother, our cat Hurricane, and my older brother Alan. Ian was still in the hospital, and Colin was off serving in the Fleet Air Arm. Back then, we were called the Greenfields – my father's family name. I even registered at school under that name, Joy Greenfield.

Not long after, our name was changed to MacRae. I remember how confusing that was, not just for me but also for the other children. Suddenly, I had to get used to being called by another name. It all felt so strange, like I wasn't quite myself but playing a part in someone else's story.

It was a bit of a legal hassle, too, because it required a deed poll, a document that proved my new name and my identity, especially when the name on my birth certificate didn't match the name on the marriage certificate. Over the years, I have used that deed poll many times. It has been sent with applications for Canadian pensions and benefits.

I remember holding it in my hands, a worn, sepia-toned paper so old and delicate that it could barely be read anymore. It looked like something from another time, stained by age, from a distant chapter of my life.

Now, at ninety years old, I still have that worn paper. I have just submitted it once more, this time for my next British passport. Life keeps moving forward, and so does that little slip of paper that quietly reminds me of my childhood.

Back then, at school, the name change was nothing more than a brief nine-day wonder. It quickly faded from the children's minds as they moved on to other fleeting curiosities. We weren't the only poor family around. Some people had a little more, but many of us were struggling just to get by.

When Ian finally came home from the hospital, he began to work, and that meant extra pennies in the jar, however little they were. Mum kept busy taking every little job she could find, always trying to give us a more stable home life.

When we moved to Wivenhoe, mum applied for a rented Council house, which was common in England at the time. These council homes were everywhere. Low-income families went on a long list to get a rental house when one became available. Mum was told she probably wouldn't get one because she wasn't supported by a man; she was a single mother, even though she was still technically married to my father.

We saw newcomers arrive and quickly move into a Council house just because they lived together as husband and wife.

In those days, the system was discriminatory and unfair – one without the protections and rights we'd come to expect.

In the 1940s and 1950s, mum kept getting overlooked due to her single-mother status. We had no rights and mum barely made ends meet. Yet, we had no other choice but to continue living in our small, run-down terrace house and make the most of what we had, learning to accept the hand life dealt us.

Our neighbours were a peculiar group of people. One woman, in particular, lived with her family. She was a heavy drinker, and most nights she staggered home from the pub. She always kept her head bowed down, her hands shoved deep in her coat pockets, but if we were outside and she saw us, her eyes would glance sideways and acknowledge us when we said 'Hello.' There was often noise and shouting when she got home. Her husband resented having to babysit their daughter every night.

She always seemed pregnant, but she was not. She just had a very large stomach on a painfully thin body. Sometimes she had a black eye after a violent argument with her husband, but strangely, neither the police nor anyone else ever intervened. We shrugged it off then. Her young daughter was mischievous beyond her years. I remember thinking even then that she probably just craved attention. Years later, I met her again and was surprised to find she was a lovely and kind woman.

Next door, an older man, his wife, and their daughter lived. The daughter was a spinster of sorts, but I remember meeting her cousin from Brentwood during a visit. That cousin wrote to me after he returned home, and I still remember the letter as it was so poorly spelled that it was proof enough that he had no real chance of winning my heart. English was my best subject, and anyone who couldn't spell was definitely not going to be considered.

The old man next door was a dirty old man, and his toilet was right behind ours. I swear, we knew every time he farted. He always wore a captain's hat in the house as well as in the garden, and we never saw him without it during the years we lived next door. He was one major reason I was constipated in my youth. The noise from his toilet whenever he had a bowel movement was something I could never get used to, and the smell was even worse. It made me hold back my own movements longer than I should have, trying to avoid the whole ordeal until I got to school. The cold winters and frozen toilet system did not help encourage my bowel movements at home either.

We lived right in the middle of the row. There was a woman I never saw clearly but often wondered about. She was quite old, and someone was always coming in to look after her. I imagined her lying awake at night, listening to the loud arguments of her neighbours, wishing for peace.

To our right was a kind family whose wife was always cheerful and was the first person in our row to get a television. I remember how we would gather outside their window, craning our necks to watch through the glass as if it were a miracle. This couple were good neighbours and showed kindness to my mother, though they didn't know much about caring for chickens. Eventually, they decided to get one anyway. I named him Cecil Abner, but everyone called him CecAb for short.

The poor bird had to live in an old pram turned on its side in their yard, a makeshift shelter. Watching CecAb shivering in that little contraption broke my heart. It wasn't long before his tiny, peculiar cluck grew weaker, and I knew he had died from the cold. I will always remember that heartrending sound, a pathetic little peep that stuck with me. Because I had named him myself, I felt I had a special bond with CecAb and would quietly cuddle him whenever I passed his pram.

At the very end of the row lived an elderly couple whose house and garden were always impeccably clean and tidy. In the very first house on the lane lived a quiet couple whose names I never learned. Next to number one was the old slaughterhouse, which once gave our lane the name Blood Alley before it was renamed Blythe's Lane. To me, the name was fitting because the environment felt haunted by ghosts and a bit spooky, or at least it felt that way to me. I was always afraid of the slightest noise or things that went bump in the night.

Further up toward the High Street, two families lived side by side. One of the girls there was 14-years-old and pregnant with her father's child. It was a sad situation. The boy next door had twisted legs and a disturbing presence about him that I sensed even then.

Four of the houses in our row shared a tap because we did not have running water. And a brick wall separated the yards between houses four and five, adding to the feeling that we were all somehow boxed in.

There was one silver lining: we didn't worry much about security back then. We never once locked our doors. Mail was just tossed in carelessly, often early in the morning, so fortunately it didn't land on the gas ring near the front door, which was connected to the gas metre. I remember Jack the postman well. He was a robust man with a big smile who would come early and throw the mail in. No matter what I was doing, I knew he would come, and he taught me about trust, routine, and community.

At Christmas, we gave him a tot, a strong alcoholic drink. By the end of his route that day, Jack walked in a wobbly fashion, dragging his bag behind his bike.

Smells and Insects and Lessons from a Hard Childhood

Our house was constantly filled with its own persistent smells that lingered from days and years gone by. On washing day, the scent of wet clothes would fill the air, heavy and damp, clinging to every corner. When mum cooked sausages and onions – something we ate often – the house was thick with the scent of caramelized onions, sticky and smoky. When mum brought fish home from her job at the factory, the raw fishy stench lingered long after. If the boys wet their beds, the house absorbed the sour smell of urine, and mum would spend hours trying to dry the stained sheets that hung over chairs, hoping they'd be dry enough to use that night.

Mum and I slept in the front bedroom. Like her mother, she was terrified of the dark, and she kept a paraffin lamp lit all night; its smoky flames had a dancing shadow that added a ghostly presence to the room. The smell of burning paraffin mingled with the smoke curling up and leaving a dull, smoky patch on the ceiling.

The house was infested with insects. The large harvest spiders that lurked in the toilet and crept across the walls could be as big as four inches across their hairy bodies. Seeing one above your head was enough to make your heart stop, and I would pray fervently that it wouldn't fall on me. One day, I looked up and saw one fall at my feet, its legs twitching. I screamed and jumped back, instinct taking over, and I had to squash it despite my fear. Today, I think I would have just opened the door and let it scuttle outside.

We knew mice were everywhere because we could see their droppings in every closet, every cupboard, little dark pellets that told us we weren't alone. I was never really afraid of mice. As a child, I caught many of them and cornered them behind piles of dishes or other objects, picked them up gently and took them outside. Hurricane, our cat, was their fiercest enemy, and he spent his days chasing mice in the house and garden and played with them as if they were toys. Watching him stalk and pounce was entertaining.

But the cockroaches were a different story. They were vile and frightening, especially at night when they came in swarms from their hiding spots beneath the floorboards and behind the fireplace. During the day, they disappeared and mercifully left us alone. The first time we discovered a group of them was after an evening out. We returned to a dark house, and when I turned on the light, the floor was a living, writhing mass of cockroaches rushing for cover. As a game, we would try to spot the most before they vanished. Cockroaches are hateful creatures, almost impossible to kill, and seem to thrive on insect sprays and all of our attempts to rid our home of them.

One moment with the cockroaches haunts me still. It was a humiliating experience that sealed my aversion forever. I had invited a boy I liked to our home for tea and made a salmon salad from canned salmon, little sandwiches, and trifle. While waiting for him to arrive, I covered the dishes with netting, weighed down by beads that we used to cover our milk jug and sugar basin. When this boy arrived, I proudly put my dishes on the table and lifted the cover. There was an ugly cockroach smugly sitting right on top of the salmon salad. I was mortified. I threw out the dish immediately, feeling my cheeks burn with shame. I couldn't face him after that.

It was another romance out the window.

That was the last time I invited anyone over for tea while we lived at that house, and we lived there for 15 years. It would be a cold day in hell before I exposed myself to that embarrassment again. From our home, I learned that life is messy, sometimes filled with smells and creatures that can make you feel small and helpless. But even in the midst of ugliness, there can be moments of strength and humour that shine through.

Hand-made toys

I can still see the little pink rabbit with a bulbous body that seemed to bounce with its roundness. It's funny how certain toys stay with you, not just because of what they are, but because of what they represent – the simple, handmade love poured into them and the roughness of the materials, which held many memories during hard times.

As a child, I remember only having one or two of these toys, but each one felt like a treasure. They were precious gifts carefully crafted with patience by my aunty.

My aunty, who made these toys, knew how to create Scotty dogs with little pointed ears, sewn-on whiskers, and buttons for eyes. They were made from old towels, blankets, coats, and any material that could be recycled into something new.

She had a talent for making toys that looked almost alive. One Christmas morning, I found this Scotty handmade dog nestled in my stocking, along with a shiny shilling from my mother, an orange, and an apple tucked carefully in the toe.

There was one year I received a football, but it was no ordinary ball. It was a heavy, solid thing, almost like a brick, without any air inside. Made from strips of cloth wound tightly and stitched together, it was almost impossible to lift off the ground. We would throw this soccer ball in the air with all our might, dodging and ducking as it whizzed towards us, a deadly weapon. Kicking it was a sure way to bruise toes, so we didn't kick, no, we tossed, we threw, we dodged.

Later, my mother made me a doll. However, it was the ugliest doll I had ever seen. It bore no resemblance to the delicate Shirley Temple doll I had longed for, which I had seen in a shop window and thought was so beautiful and perfect. My mother's doll had straight wool hair that seemed as if it hadn't been brushed in years, a flat face with an embroidered nose, eyes, and mouth that looked more like stitched scars. Its body and limbs were made from a dish towel, stuffed with bits of rag and scraps of fabric.

The dress was knitted from unravelled wool that once belonged to one of my old jumpers from the charity shop. How I wished with all my heart for the Shirley Temple doll, something shiny and perfect and new. But it was not to be. The doll my mother made was neither new nor beautiful, and certainly not what I had dreamed of. It was just another reminder of how scarce resources were, and how love sometimes had to be spun from the tiniest bits of hope. I never did find another doll to fill its place.

CHAPTER 13

Girl Gangs and Coming of Age

Growing up in that small village in Wivenhoe, life was often influenced by the girl gang that ruled the primary school. They seemed fixated on sex – whether it was to do with themselves or everyone else. Perhaps there was nothing else happening in the village to occupy them. This gang of rough girls targeted the more timid girls, those who seemed to shrink under their scrutiny and relentless bullying. As a new girl in the village, I was an easy target. I was small, didn't have a father living with us, and lived in a crumbling, condemned house that seemed to draw attention for all the wrong reasons. That combination made me stand out in all the wrong ways.

The bullying started almost as soon as I arrived. Recess became a living nightmare, a daily battle I dreaded. I tried to stay indoors, hide away in the classroom, but teachers, perhaps with good intentions, would send me outside to play and get some fresh air. The teachers turned a blind eye and never seemed to notice what was happening on the playground. I understand now that nobody told them about the girl gang and the bullying that was going on; therefore, they couldn't intervene. I can't really blame them.

The violence was rough. At first, it was punches to my arms, legs, anywhere they could land them after being segregated from the other girls and pinned against the cold, metal rails or the rough brick walls.

Things only got worse. I remember being cornered in the girls' toilets, forced to sit on the cold tiled floor, my pants pulled down so they could see and mock me. It was all wrapped up in this sick obsession with sex. It was a cruel way for those girls to establish dominance by instilling terror. They fixated on breasts, real or developing, and on my body hair. They would do this to other girls. They wanted us to report every new hair as if it was some kind of great new discovery.

When I got my first period, I thought it might be something to celebrate. It was a sign I was growing up, after all. Fortunately, the gang's interest in me would shift after my period started, and they had no further interest in looking at my so-called family jewels.

These memories are raw and sometimes hard to face, but they are part of who I am, and I've become stronger because of these experiences.

I didn't grow up knowing much about sex or sexuality. It was never discussed at home. At school, there was chatter, not openly but in hushed whispers, about what was possible, what some girls might be experimenting with. It wasn't until the Americans came to town and attended the local dances that some of the local girls told tales of oral sex favoured by the American troops. It was a revelation to us who had never heard of this forbidden knowledge before. That opened my eyes to a wider world I was barely beginning to understand.

The American troops were excellent dancers. They taught us how to jive and rock and roll. I never went out with any of them, even though many stayed at the old Manor house in the park, which is now part of Essex University. I remember visiting the park before the Americans moved in. The grounds were beautiful, lush and inviting. As children, we would explore, playing hide-and-seek among the trees, feeling free to roam in a way children rarely do now.

The house belonged to the Gooches then, and we spent many hours wandering freely, revelling in the simple joy of childhood with no worries, no fears, just the thrill of being out until dark, when it was time to go home. We always knew the rule: be home before dark. That rule kept us safe.

I remember once visiting the Gooch house, where the visiting American troops were stationed. My older brother Colin had just returned home on leave and took me there. I was young and eager to see this mysterious house, even if it meant trespassing. He somehow managed to get us in – I still wonder how he pulled it off, because Colin was a master liar with a poker face that could fool anyone. Somehow, I believed he could talk his way into that house and through anything.

I was very well developed at 10 and had entered puberty early. Having periods made me feel like I was a magnet for the opposite sex, though at the time, I only understood it as being different from other kids.

I was about to leave primary school when I turned eleven. Back then, the plan was simple. If I could pass an exam, I'd move on to high school. If I didn't, I'd have to stay at the secondary school in Brightlingsea, which was only about six miles away and yet felt like a whole different world.

In the end, I didn't pass the exam at eleven years old. It was a disappointment, but I didn't give up even when it seemed like an impossible goal. I managed to pass that exam when I was thirteen. Even now, these memories remind me of how far I've come and how much I have achieved since then.

CHAPTER 14

The Musical MacRaes

I didn't grow up with a television in the house. Our neighbours did, though, and I remember how special it felt to be invited over to watch a program – in black and white, of course. Television was such a novelty and a marvel to us back then, a shiny new thing we knew we would never be able to afford ourselves. In those days, it was as if that simple act of sitting together to watch a show was a huge deal.

I still cherish the memory of the first time we got a radio. We were entranced by the music programs we could listen to, as well as serials like Dick Barton, Special Agent. I can still see all the children rushing home at exactly 7 pm, eager to listen to our favourite adventure on Dick Barton. Before we had a radio, or even after, we found other ways to amuse ourselves. There were no computers, no Nintendo or Xbox, no shiny, fancy toys from the store to distract us. Instead, we used our imagination. We made up games, sang, and crafted toys from cardboard, cotton reels, tin cans, string, and anything else we could find. In those days, we learned to entertain ourselves, to think for ourselves.

Music was at the heart of those childhood years and our main amusement. We were all 'into it,' and it became our passion. My mother was a remarkable pianist. She played with a talent that seemed almost otherworldly. I remember her practising late into the night, her hands gliding effortlessly across the keys. She was so skilled, she was invited to train with a master. I never quite understood what that meant at the time, but I knew it must have been something extraordinary, perhaps like studying at Juilliard. She was of concert calibre, and I often wondered how different her life could have been if her parents had allowed her to pursue her music full-time and become a concert pianist. Sadly, they could not afford to pay for her to study piano away from home.

She was disciplined and dedicated. Whenever she could steal a moment, she would sit at the piano and play, lost in her music. In her quiet way, she kept that love alive.

When we moved to Wivenhoe, our home didn't have a piano. I could see how much she missed having one. But she was determined. She managed to find an old, battered piano. It was a real old clunker and mum bought it for just one shilling, the same amount we paid in weekly rent for the house. When we brought that old thing home, her eyes lit up with joy. She was so excited, so grateful. That piano, despite its worn-out appearance, became her prized possession. She loved it with a fierce tenderness, and I watched her, understanding even then that that simple instrument meant everything to her. It was a link to her talent, her dreams, and a part of herself she refused to let go.

We all had to go and get the old upright piano from the previous owner. My three brothers and I went together and felt a sense of dread. Moving that piano wasn't easy. It was heavy and bulky, and getting it out of the house and onto the dirt path was a chore. Luckily, it had casters on the bottom, which made pushing it along the uneven ground possible, but it still took a lot of effort. When we reached Blythe's Lane, the task became even harder. The road there was just gravel and no pavement, which turned the push into a struggle over rough, loose stones. It was tough work, but somehow we managed to get it into the house, where mum was waiting for us with a proud smile.

The piano was an old upright and was out of tune. Mum found a blind man who could tune pianos perfectly. He came to our house and carefully adjusted each string. We watched in fascination as he worked, every turn of his wrench making the sound richer and clearer. When he finished, the piano sounded so much better and roared with a new life. Mum sat down on the nearby chair, gently ran her fingers over the keys, and smiled. She said she would teach me how to play. I remember feeling a warmth spread through me, even though the house was cold and my fingers were always numb. I complained that I couldn't learn because of my cold fingers, and I didn't persevere. Now I wish I had. If I had known then what I know now, I would have practised, paid attention, and taken her lessons seriously. Mum would have given me free lessons, which I didn't take advantage of.

I would have loved to sit at that piano and learn from her, to make some music of my own. Sometimes I wonder what it would have been like to be able to play well, to really feel the notes vibrating through me.

Ah, 20/20 hindsight. Later on, I finally took some piano lessons as an adult, and maybe I will do it again someday.

What I do know is that I had a decent singing voice. I could hold a tune, and singing helped me escape and forget all my worries and shyness. It made me forget about being poor and feeling like I didn't belong. Mum encouraged me from an early age, asking me to sing for the family during quiet Sunday afternoons. Those moments linger in my memory as some of the happiest times.

During Sunday afternoons in Wivenhoe, mum would sit at the piano and play classical pieces. I couldn't sing along with most of them because they were too complicated. Instead, I encouraged her to play popular songs from that time, songs I could sing to and feel connected to. We would have little concerts right there in our humble home, with the neighbours sometimes gathered outside the window listening in. We'd push the window open so they could lean in and get a better look, as if they were part of our simple, imperfect family show. They were our first concert audiences! It was just us dreaming of better days to come, holding onto moments of happiness.

My brothers each played an instrument, and all of them were self-taught from the start. Colin was a very good pianist, his fingers moving across the keys with a natural grace. He also played the harmonica and guitar, often picking up whichever instrument was at hand with an enthusiasm that was contagious. Colin was a talented artist, too. He was especially creative in needlework and embroidery, which was so unusual for a man in those days. He was also a very talented oil painter and created art that was quite striking.

Ian played the guitar, though he wasn't very good at it. Still, he had a gift for the harmonica and preferred it, sometimes blowing out soulful notes. Ian was good on the drums, although he did not own his own set. He played only when he could borrow someone else's drums. He loved boogie-woogie piano and had a collection of records of the genre. He also admired Beniamino Gigli, the famous opera singer of his time. Ian tried to play the guitar, but he faked most of it, too lazy to really learn properly.

Alan played the guitar, banjo, harmonica, and ukulele. He was the most talented of us all when it came to music. Listening to him play the banjo was like hearing a real bluegrass band right in our living room. He went on to become a folk singer and made some records. He started his career working as a social worker for the Catholic Children's Aid Society, which tells you something about his caring nature. Eventually, he left that work behind to devote himself full-time to singing and songwriting. I wish I hadn't lost track of his albums. I once lent them to someone and never got them back. They disappeared somewhere along the way, lost to me forever.

Joy's brother Alan is holding the banjo in this photo with his band, The Chanteclairs, on their record cover in 1962.

Joy's mother with Alan celebrating his record's success in 1962 in a Canadian newspaper clipping.

Our mother was the biggest supporter of all our musical pursuits. She encouraged us in every way she could. Before long, the boys would sit at the piano with her, playing along as she played beautiful melodies.

Voila, a band was born!

Alan had a kind of raw artistic talent that went beyond music. He was a gifted singer, a talented artist, and even an actor. His creativity seemed boundless, and he approached everything with an innate sense of style.

We often played as a family at local events and when Ian strummed what he called a one-note chord at local dances, the village kids would gather around, eager for a demonstration. Ian would shoot them a sidewise hiss out of the side of his mouth and tell them to get lost.

Singing at the local dances was where I first found my love for the stage. Despite being painfully shy and tongue-tied most of the time, I sang because it made me feel alive. Turning fifty gave me the courage to join Toastmasters and learn how to speak out. I discovered I had a voice I could use, a voice I could trust. That moment changed everything. I eventually became a professional speaker and continued singing in bands and choirs for the rest of my life.

Colin was able to pick up almost anything he set his mind to, whether it was sewing, knitting, painting, decorating, or music. I remember him once transforming the inside of our house in Wivenhoe into something that looked like a castle. The walls were painted with battlements, and there was a princess hanging out of a window, waiting for her rescue. There was a drawbridge and a moat, a knight in shining armour, and a winding road leading up to the castle gates. He turned our backroom into something spectacular, far beyond what I ever imagined possible for us.

Colin also painted the ward where he worked as a male nurse after he left the Fleet Air Arm. He decorated the ward for children and he poured his heart into turning it into a fairyland. He also crafted a five-foot teddy bear, with arms and legs that moved, to sit in the ward for the children to play with. Colin also crafted a doll resembling Red Riding Hood, entirely out of felt. He gave her bright blue eyes that shone like tiny sapphires, blonde, curly hair that looked soft enough to touch, and a beautiful red cloak over a pretty white dress that seemed to glow. The doll's red hood was just right, framing her delicate face.

That doll was like a dream from my childhood, something I had longed for but never got. I remember how I wanted her fiercely when I was little, but my brother forbade me from touching her. He said he didn't want her to get dirty. I was not supposed to have her, but when he wasn't home, I would sneak her out of her box, pretending she was mine altogether. I would set up tiny tea parties for her, making her sit at a little table, her face level with the table's edge. She was well-mannered, and I would spoon little bits of rice pudding into her perfect little rosebud mouth, imagining she was alive and enjoying it just like I did.

Imagine my horror, one day, when a piece of rice pudding slipped and fell onto her red cape. 'Oh no,' I cried (I didn't swear in those days). I scrubbed at the stain with a wet facecloth, but it only seemed to make things worse. My heart pounded fiercely in my chest as I hurried to hide her away, feeling a terrible weight of guilt.

I was sure that my naughtiness showed up on my face. I felt helpless and sorry for ruining a doll that I wanted so badly. The very next day, my brother saw the stain and took the doll to work with him. I never saw her again after that. I was pained by the loss of something precious.

Not long after that, he showed up back home with a wife in tow, a girl he had met at work and married without telling my mother. My mother and I had to pack our things and move out of the front bedroom. We ended up sleeping downstairs on a pull-out Chesterfield in the front room, while Colin and Paddy, as she was called, took over our old bedroom upstairs. Colin was a talented artist, but he was also a pathological liar and shared wild stories he seemed to believe himself.

He told Paddy that we were rich, that I was a ballerina, and that my mother was a concert pianist. Such lies. I never knew how Paddy felt when she found out we were dirt poor. I have wondered whether those lies hurt her.

Paddy and Colin stayed with us for quite a while, until they moved into a Nissan Hut in the town of Messing in Essex. Colin, despite his many flaws, decorated the inside of that Nissan Hut with real care and a sense of beauty, turning it into a stunning home that was far more inviting than the house he had left behind.

Sadly, those two fought all the time. They argued like cats and dogs. I remember once visiting and seeing Paddy throw a can of red paint at Colin. It didn't hit him, but it did mess up his careful decorating. Watching them, I saw that love and hatred could often be two sides of the same coin.

When Colin left the Fleet Air Arm, he brought home the company mascot dog. Sandy was a golden retriever – a lovely dog – and was immediately loved by the village children. Every morning, he went out alone and returned with a collection of items, such as pieces of laundry, a boot, or a shoe. We then had to find the owners of these articles.

Sandy often accompanied mum on her shopping trips, carrying a bag in his mouth for her. He also went with her and us to fetch coal. When Colin moved to Messing, he took Sandy with him. It broke my heart because I loved that dog. He used to come with me when I went out with the local children.

Shortly after they moved, I heard that Sandy had been shot by a gamekeeper for trespassing. I knew Colin to be a liar and never believed him, but I missed his dog.

Colin and his wife adopted a Polish baby, and over time, they had two more children of their own. Later, they moved to John's Wood in London, where they bought a Saint Bernard dog. I remember walking that dog a few times when I visited. It would sit down on a zebra crossing, and I'd need to get help to shift it. Eventually, they relocated to Liverpool, where they fostered and adopted vulnerable youngsters.

Our music in Wivenhoe carried on until 1958, when we emigrated to Canada. Alan became a musician, performing with a group called The Chanticlairs. Unfortunately, he also fell into the drinking lifestyle some performers indulge in, which ultimately claimed his life at just 50.

I, too, became a performer, singing lead vocals with a band. I recorded a few CDs and I continue to perform and I plan to keep singing as long as I can.

Those moments of creativity and music helped us survive a challenging childhood. Talent can flourish in the most unlikely places, and perseverance can turn simple skills into something extraordinary.

Music CD covers featuring Joy as a singer in a band between 2008 to 2015.

CHAPTER 15

Mother's Dresses

When mum packed the trunk for the shelter in 1938, she included two dresses she had worn as a Military Officer's wife in China, Egypt, and India, along with the dancing shoes she wore with them. I was glad she had kept the dresses, but I never quite understood why she held onto them. I imagine she couldn't bear to part with such lovely clothes. Now, I have similar dresses in my own closet, and I understand that same reluctance to let go of something beautiful, even if I have no use for it. Over time, I've come to terms with it and now regularly donate clothes to charity.

As a child, mum's dresses attracted me like a magnet to the wardrobe where she kept them. I often imagined how incredible it must have felt to be dressed in that 1920s splendour. I loved to wear them and pretend I was whirling around a dance floor in the arms of a handsome boy. My imagination was my best friend and it carried me away from the reality we lived in.

One of the dresses was pink, with ruffles from top to bottom. Mum had also kept a long string of white beads, which seemed to perfectly match the dress – very much in the style of the 20's. This was my favourite dress-up gown. Wearing it, I could imagine myself to be anyone I wanted to be. I was about nine then and the dress was way too big for me. However, I'd tie it in place with a piece of string so it wouldn't drag on the floor, and retreat into my own fantasy world. I'd slip my tiny feet into elegant dancing shoes and shuffle around the bedroom, feeling absolutely glamorous.

The pink dress hadn't been worn for nearly twenty years and had a faint musty smell, which was not surprising, but I didn't mind. I imagined myself elegantly holding a long cigarette holder, wearing a beaded headband, with a dashing escort taking me to the Gatsby party in his Edsel car. I'd imagine us doing the Charleston, feet and legs flashing, tassels and fringes swaying, bodies twisting and dipping to the music.

When I opened my eyes and saw my face in the mirror, it brought me back down to earth with a sudden thud.

I played with that dress until it wasn't fit to wear, and I had outgrown that stage of pretending. The other purple dress mum saved was more glam than the pink ruffles. More about that later. We found a use for it.

CHAPTER 16

Sunday Best

I was brought up with the philosophy that good things, like clothes, fine china, and tablecloths, had to be saved for special occasions. Even in some houses, rooms were left unused unless visitors arrived; typically, the front room was cold and unheated. When visitors came, the fire would be lit.

If we were lucky enough to have a good coat and shoes, we saved them for Sunday, when we went to Church and then took a walk afterwards. The walk allowed us to keep our best clothes on for a bit longer.

I was very careful to sidestep puddles and dog feces when wearing my good patent leather shoes. When we got home, they were placed back in their box, with only a little road dust on them. My coat would be hung in the narrow cupboard, protected by mothballs to guard it from the ever-present and very hungry moths.

Next Sunday, the same thing would happen. The coat and shoes would see the light of day for a few hours. The shoes would be wiped over with a thin layer of Vaseline to make them shine. I wore them with little white ankle socks and my best coat. The clothes and shoes mum managed to get were always paid for in instalments. We would pick what we wanted from a catalogue, pay a deposit, and then pay the item off in instalments. I got most of my clothes that way while growing up. Mum was good at setting aside a little money to buy us decent clothes from local shops. Catalogue buying was very popular, though, and most people we knew used them.

I took good care of the coats that I had as a child. The first one I remember was beige with a brown velvet collar and nice pockets. I loved that coat. When I outgrew it, mum got me an oatmeal-coloured coat, flared with gores, buttons up to the neck, and a stand-up collar. I felt very special wearing it.

One day, at school, it was announced that there would be a trip for the class to the British Museum in London. I didn't have to pay for it as our family grant covered it. The grant paid for train fares and admission to the Museum. I found it very exciting. I wanted to wear my coat.

The night before the trip, mum wound my straight, platinum-blond hair into ringlets. To do this, she soaked the hair in sugar water and then wound it around rags, which were tied at the bottom after being wound from bottom to top and top to bottom. I had to hold one end of each rag while mum wound the other end. The rags were always tied tightly and the hair pulled at the scalp. Sleeping on these rag-wrapped ringlets was pure torture, but I endured it, because I wanted to look my very best.

Morning arrived after a painfully sleepless night. The rags were unwrapped and removed. Voila! I found myself with a head full of tight sausage ringlets – impossible to comb because the sugar in the water held the ringlets together like superglue! It wasn't meant to be like that!

After several failed attempts to tame the ringlets, I wrapped a scarf around my head, put on my lovely coat, and headed to the station, eager to travel to London by train. The train steamed in. Some children were already aboard, as it had come from Clacton and Brightlingsea, and some of my classmates were from those areas.

The steam trains were powered by coal, so there was smoke in the air and it was generally dirty. Hanging our hands out the window while the smoke blew back was a neat trick, but it left our hands very dirty.

I was about nine and had small breasts. My period was to start before I was 10 years old. My little bumps were a magnet for the boys, and coupled with the 'posh' ringlets, it was just too much for those cool boys. I was grabbed from behind. While one held my arms, another one placed his dirty hands on the outside of my lovely coat, in the vicinity of my little budding breasts.

I screamed. A teacher came running, but she was too late to save my lovely coat. The black handprints were there for all to see.

The day turned into a nightmare after that. It started with me feeling proud of my lovely coat and a head full of sausage ringlets. It ended with me crying and miserable over my ruined coat. I never wore it again. Mum couldn't remove the black handprints. I refused to wear it with the shameful marks on it.

Fortunately, I grew older, and more coats followed. One was a beige coat with a pleated back, another was a light green, smartly belted, and my overall favourite was a blue tweed with large patch pockets. I loved that one with an intensity the others couldn't match. Still, I held a special place in my heart for the ruined oatmeal-coloured coat I had when I was nine.

I have always loved coats and have had a lifelong passion for stylish ones. I loved the black swagger purchased in Montreal, the white leather one with fox fur trim, the white wool with fur trimmings, the three-piece raincoat with a fur collar and a fur vest that zipped out, and the Linda Lundström purple parka. I loved them all and still do.

I once bought a full-length white coat made of Mongolian goat fur. When I turned 50, my husband decided I should have a full-length raccoon fur coat for the Ontario winters. More on fashion later.

I remembered the Sunday Best ritual from when my children were growing up. My philosophy was that we shouldn't wait for a special occasion to wear nice things or to use the best china. Use everything every day. Tomorrow might not come. We enjoyed using everything while we had it. When it broke or wore out, we moved on and used something else. We used the good china every day. I still do. Nothing is saved for a rainy day.

Every room in our home has its purpose and I never sit politely in the chilly front rooms. Instead, I have a fire burning in the grate to chase away the cold. When it's cold outside, our fire is alive, the wine is poured into our finest crystal glasses, and I wear my best outfits whenever the mood strikes. Life is too short to save things for a rainy day – every day should be cherished as something special.

CHAPTER 17

The Beauty Contest

When I look back on my childhood in Wivenhoe, I remember the local Youth Club as a lively hub of my young life. It was a place brimming with energy, where I could meet up with other kids, meet boys, learn to dance, and participate in musical shows and various events. One event stands out in my memory. It was the Beauty Contest, the only one I ever entered.

I was just 12 when the club announced the contest, open to girls up to age 14. I was desperate to take part, even though deep down I knew I didn't have much of a chance. I was shy and felt out of place among the village girls who seemed so confident and polished. To my untrained eye, they were pretty and sophisticated, many of them having already slept with the American soldiers passing through. I was still a virgin, still innocent.

I had started my period when I was nearly 10, and I knew some of the less developed girls hadn't yet had theirs or had period pain. Back then, every girl's ambition was to have her first period and join the club of women, but I viewed it differently. I wished I didn't have my period and would have been only too happy to give my period away to the others. Sadly, that was not possible. The truth was, I was envious of those who didn't have their periods and a little bewildered by what I was going through.

Even though I had achieved what many of the girls hadn't, I still didn't feel attractive. I saw myself as a chubby child, with everyone else appearing prettier than me. All I wanted was to be like everyone else. I longed to do what they did, discussing what to wear for the contest. I deeply resented being poor. I knew mum didn't have the money to buy me a dress for this Beauty Contest. Perhaps aunty Ada would make me something.

I hated feeling like the odd one out, always on the outside looking in. Most villagers had lived there their entire lives, so they were very familiar with everyone. Newcomers, like me, were strangers and needed time to fit in. I never understood that you couldn't rush the process.

I was shy, and on top of that, poor and unattractive. My shyness stemmed from a gap in my front teeth. We didn't have a dentist until I was in my teens, when they finally fixed it. Before that, I rarely smiled.

When I told my mother about the contest, her face showed doubt.

"Why would you want to enter?" she asked.

"I just want to. All the girls are going to," I replied. I didn't want to be left out. I simply wanted to do what everyone else was doing.

Mum thought for a moment and then said the only thing she had that could be turned into a dress for me was her purple satin evening gown. It was the second best dress, the one from her past life, that was packed away in the old trunk.

"Maybe aunty Ada can turn it into a dress for you," she said.

I was overjoyed to hear her say that. I hadn't worn that stunning dress when I was playing dress up. It was a one-shoulder dress and it must have been very sexy in the 1920s when she wore it. I didn't care what it had been, only what it would become for me. I was actually going to be able to enter this contest.

It must have been difficult for her to give up a part of her cherished past, though I hadn't thought about that at the time. Now, I understand she made a personal sacrifice for me.

I had never seen mum in the dress. The satin was very slinky and shiny, the back very low to the waist, the one strap draped over the shoulder and flowed to the waist.

"There's plenty of material to make a dress for you," she said softly, running her hands over the material.

So off we went to aunty Ada's house with the dress in a bag. I enjoyed visiting her because she always had biscuits for me. She was one of the kindest people I had ever known, always gentle and smiling. She and uncle Ernie lived in a small, terraced house in Colchester. Uncle Ernie was mum's brother. He and Ada had a very romantic story. Ada had been a novice nun, just about to become a Bride of Christ, when she met Ernie. They fell madly in love. Ada left the Nunnery, but her faith remained intact. They adored each other and felt no need to have children. When he died of throat cancer, she died not long afterwards of bladder cancer. I always thought she died of a broken heart.

On this day, she laid out the purple satin dress on the table, measured me, and started cutting. She hummed happily while snipping away, a gentle smile on her face as she worked. It was so sweet of aunty Ada to do this for me, and she didn't complain once. I thought it was because she used to be a nun, and that's just how a Bride of Christ would act: kind and gentle.

Two weeks later, we went to pick up the dress. Aunty Ada had designed a simple sundress with a halter neck. The back was open all the way down to the waist, with the halter looping around my neck. It reached my knees and had a full, flowing skirt. I felt so grown-up and elegant in that purple, slinky dress.

On the day of the contest, mum curled my hair with rags again. This time, I used water to tame the sausage curls a bit and flattened them. We didn't have a full-length mirror, so I couldn't see myself. Mum said I looked great, and I felt pretty special. The dress fit me like it was made for me. It should have had a bra under it, but I didn't own one. My 32C breasts fit it quite nicely.

Finally, it was the day of the Beauty Contest and I was nervous. I put my coat over my dress and headed up the High Street to the Youth Centre. The place was full of parents settling into the audience. The Youth Director was organizing the contestants on the side of the stage. They were lined up. I felt a little panic when I noticed they were all wearing white dresses, some with frilly patterns and even frillier petticoats, hair arranged in smooth curls with cute bows. My hair was in sausage ringlets, thanks to the rag method.

Most of the girls had nylons on their legs and some had lipstick on and rouge on their faces. I was the only one in a backless purple dress, which made me clutch my coat a little tighter.

I quietly took my place in the line and looked down at my plain shoes and socks. I should have borrowed mum's dancing shoes, which she had put into the chest. They were probably too big for me. I could hear the announcer now, asking everyone to be quiet, then he explained the rules to the audience.

"Applaud for the one you like the best," he said. "The one who gets the most applause wins the prize, which is to be Queen of the Youth Club for the next year."

The girl who won this was sure to be the most popular girl at the dances. She would not have to sit out a single dance at the Youth Club Dances in the Village Hall. I loved these dances, but to be honest, I did sit out a few of them. I liked to dance with Alan from school. We were teaching each other how to dance. He was a good dancer, thanks to me, and the girls liked dancing with him because of it.

The first girl stepped onto the stage. She was a pretty girl and received quite a lot of applause. I was starting to get anxious and my coat still concealed my almost bare skin. I knew I would have to take it off soon because the line was moving quite well now. Sometimes the applause was lengthy, and other times it was just polite clapping.

My turn came and I shrugged off my coat and stepped onto the stage. I heard a gasp – an intake of accumulated breaths. It was audible; a group gasp as they beheld me in all my purple magnificence! The announcer said my name and how I wished he had not done that, but left me anonymous. I wanted the stage to open up and swallow me. I wished to be suddenly struck dead. I wished I could swoon and be carried off by a handsome prince. I couldn't even summon up one of the fainting spells that had plagued me as a child. Nothing could save me from being the centre of attention, except the walk back to where my coat was.

I listened to the faint smattering of applause as I shrugged into my coat. It was polite applause, only accompanied by much louder whispering.

I realized the slinky purple dress was all wrong for this village. I was an outsider, and tonight I proved it in front of everyone. I got what I wanted: to do what they did, to be like them, but I knew I could never truly be one of them. I could only be myself, not a carbon copy of someone else.

Thinking about the embarrassment, the whispers, the nerves, the judgment, I wondered what was so great about being part of the crowd.

Quietly, I slipped out into the evening and headed home. The wind was strong, branches swayed, and leaves danced in a rhythm only they understood. I buried my face in the wind, tears rolling down my cheeks and into my curly hair as I made my way home, feeling torn up inside.

That night, I decided I'd never enter a Beauty Contest again. I've wondered if mum and aunty Ada wanted me to learn something from the experience, but I think they were just being kind. They probably didn't know how badly I'd be humiliated. I prefer to believe they knew I needed to experience it to really understand and grow from it.

Never again. It's more important to stay true to yourself rather than be a crowd-pleaser. Being authentic takes time, but it's worth the effort.

The comparisons and the feeling of not fitting in were things I was still trying to understand. Childhood was difficult, but it was also a time of quiet observation, of learning about the world and myself, often painfully so.

CHAPTER 18

Ouija Boards

Mum was very interested in the spirit world. She truly believed there were ghosts out there who appeared and spoke only to certain people. I already knew that uncle Ernie had a resident ghost in their house. He had conversations with this ghost. Ernie had also seen a ghost in a churchyard. It beckoned to him while he was walking by, but he didn't go over to it, though.

At other times, Ernie would see a man suspended over the toilet tank outside in their old privy. The toilet was the type with a tank and a chain hanging over the toilet seat. The male spirit in the toilet didn't seem evil – he was just hanging around. Maybe he died there and had nowhere else to go. I was always afraid of using this toilet when I visited uncle Ernie's home. Luckily, the ghost didn't bother them. Aunty Ada never saw any ghosts herself.

It seemed like our side of the family was more susceptible to spirits. To my young mind, I believed Ada would have special protection from evil spirits because of her close relationship with God.

Ernie also had a ghost in the spare bedroom. I wondered if it was the same one! Maybe it followed him around, flitting about whenever it felt like it. Probably not. Ernie used to say the second bedroom was really chilly, and he wouldn't go in unless he absolutely had to. Even with a fireplace, it was never warm. When I visited, I'd sneak up the stairs just to check it out. Sure enough, it was freezing, that kind of uncomfortable cold that made you wish you weren't there. The idea that I might see something spooky made my heart pound. I was terrified but also kind of fascinated.

I didn't see anything, but I always figured these ghosts were just waiting for someone willing to listen to their message. They probably sensed I didn't really believe. My closest brushes with the supernatural were when I felt my hair stand on end or a shiver run down my spine. To be totally honest though, there were two times that genuinely scared me, when I felt something evil in the air.

One was in the dark dungeons of Colchester Castle. I felt so uneasy I had to leave, rushing up the stairs to the upper levels.

The second time was in a house my friend was buying. She was showing it to me, and when she opened the cellar door, it was as if an invisible hand was holding me back. I couldn't go down those stairs or take a step forward. I felt repulsed by something I couldn't see or understand. I had to step outside and get some air and take some deep breaths. My friend ended up buying the house, but I never went back inside.

My maternal grandma once saw a ghost in a ladies' toilet. This ghost was a tall woman in black who told her, "If you take as many steps backwards as you do forward, you will be no more."

I used to listen to that story in awe as a kid. As an adult, I realized it kind of made sense. If you walked backwards, you could probably get run over or fall off a cliff, so it was actually good advice from a ghost! We often wish to have eyes in the back of our heads, but they are at the front, and we couldn't walk backwards for any length of time without disaster happening to us.

My mum's sister, aunty Rose and her husband Charlie, often talked about this advice, wondering if there was a deeper, hidden meaning.

Mum could read tea leaves and enjoyed using the Ouija board, and was genuinely interested in contacting spirits. We often held séances, with an upside-down glass that supposedly moved on its own. Mum always led those.

The board is flat with the letters of the alphabet around the edge. We'd put an upside-down glass in the centre. We turned out the lights and lit a candle to set the mood. We needed to set the right atmosphere. Everyone put an index finger on the top of the glass. The first person asked a question. When the glass started moving around the board, spelling out the answer to the question, it was very spooky and always sent a chill down my spine.

Mum usually started with the question, "Is anybody there?"

The glass would start moving and spell out YES.

"Who are you?" would be the next question. Then a name would be spelled out that meant nothing to any of us.

We assumed it was the spirit of someone who had lived in the house. We all took turns asking questions, and we always got an answer. Sometimes the answers didn't make sense, but sometimes the answers were spot on.

We wondered just how they knew the answers. Mum may have known the answers to most things about our lives in those days, so she could have been doing a little bit of manoeuvring on her own.

But how could a board answer questions that only I knew the answer to? That happened once, and it was enough to persuade me there was something mysteriously terrifying about the whole process. Eventually, I got fed up and threw the board away. I asked a question nobody could answer, and the reply was correct. Skeptics say I moved the glass, but I swear I didn't. It's still a mystery to this day. Anyway, that was enough for me. I steer clear of any methods to summon spirits. Part of me suspects there might be some real power behind it, or perhaps mum was moving the glass herself to get answers. I'll never know, but I do know it frightened me.

If you've never tried an Ouija board, just leave it alone. If it's something you enjoy doing, fine, but not at my place!!

CHAPTER 19

Fathers

Maggie arrived in the village when I was eight. We were both outsiders, so we clicked right away. Her dad was the local 'Bobby,' a police officer. He was a tall, moustached man riding around on an old iron bike. He looked quite proud as he pedalled through the village with his rain cape draped over his shoulders. The cape seemed too small to keep him dry. I wouldn't have been surprised if his knees got soaked.

Maggie's family had recently moved from Canvey Island to Wivenhoe, but they still went back there for their holidays. Her full name was Margaret Shirley Ann Williams. She had a brother named Kenneth and a little sister called Valerie.

I still have a photo of Maggie on Canvey Island, sitting in the tall grass, her hair blown across her face by the wind, her skinny arms wrapped around her knees, a big grin on her face. Maggie was tall, athletic, and beautiful, unlike my short, plump, unathletic frame, but we were still great friends. That picture of her on Canvey Island always made me want to visit the place myself. It seemed a bit exotic to me, probably similar to parts of Wivenhoe. No doubt the island had as much mud as we did around the river, with the same smells.

Maggie seemed to have the best of things. Her family had a telephone in the house for police business, and I was allowed to use it now and again, which was a big treat. Phone calls were usually made in the one phone booth in the village.

Her mother was tall, elegant, always nicely dressed, polite, and pleasant. I was a bit in awe of her dad, the 'Bobby.' He scared me a little, and even though I had nothing to feel guilty about, he always made me feel guilty. I couldn't imagine having a policeman for a dad, though I would have taken any dad back then. Not having a dad seemed awful.

I never knew how to answer when people asked about my father. What was I supposed to say? I got creative with my answers. My favourite was that he had been killed in the war. Sometimes I said he disappeared before our house was bombed. Other times, I told the truth: he had left to be with another woman. I wondered why he left; perhaps she had a stronger sex drive than mum did? He fathered 12 children – six with my mother and six with Lily, his common-law wife.

Having no father was a nuisance and a burden. Now I can see how much the absence of a father has shaped me. It was a constant ache that made me feel different from the other children, as if I were missing something essential. I couldn't miss the warmth or love I had never known from a father. I couldn't miss having fun with him, for I had never had any with him. I never had the chance to hold his hand or hear his voice. There was no laughter with him, no shared joy or comfort, only an empty gap. Mum was bitter when she talked about him and the way he had treated her. She never told me the full story, only that he had treated her badly, and I learned early not to ask too many questions.

Mum was pretty and kind, and had other chances to marry again and find happiness. There were men who might have made her happier, but she was not interested in finding anyone else. She chose to remain single, refusing to divorce. She couldn't bear the thought of giving him the satisfaction of ending their marriage, so she held on to punish him. She often took him to court whenever he failed to pay the alimony owed for their children under 16.

Supporting us was a struggle for mum because there was never enough money. I am quite sure my father lived much more comfortably than we did, despite his large second family and the periodic payments to me and my three brothers, his former family. I knew he gave lessons in Scottish country dancing, sword dancing, and bagpipes, so he had income from both his teaching and his military role. Mum must have kept informed about him and his work, because from time to time, she passed on little snippets of information about him to us.

I recall the day a bouquet of Lillies arrived at the house in Blood Alley. Mum had lost her teeth to disease. She was looking particularly bad and feeling low because she was in pain. Her cheeks were sunken, and she was at one of those points in life when things seemed very bleak indeed. She was wearing a dress that she wore every day. It was shapeless and shabby on her tiny figure. She looked as if a puff of wind would blow her away.

One day, when a knock came at the door, I was surprised to see my father standing there with his girlfriend behind him. He came to ask for a divorce, but mum said 'No' as usual. He thrust the Lillies into her hands, bought for the occasion, and sneered, "You look half dead. These can go on your grave."

She cried out, "Oh, you beast!" That was how she always referred to him, as a beast. She had no great opinion of men in general. Lily, his girlfriend, was looking on. How she could be OK with a man doing that, I have no idea, but it reflects her character. On that day, she was wearing high heels, full make-up, bright red lips, rouged cheeks and long blonde hair. She was not pretty, but she had a shapely figure.

After he threw the Lillies at mum, they left to catch the train back to London, where they lived.

It was not the last time he would request a divorce, but it was the most memorable, and the only time I got a look at Lily, his common-law wife. Mum felt that by denying him a divorce, she was exacting revenge on him, making him suffer. Yet, realistically, she suffered more than he did. Life could have been much more comfortable, easier, and brighter if she had been the one to close the door on him, opening different opportunities instead.

Eventually, mum got her dentures, and she began to look better. Her hair was neatly trimmed and permed. She managed to find nicer clothes. However, no matter what she wore or did to improve herself, she never lost the look of pain in her eyes.

The new dentures did not fit very well and often fell out when she laughed or played blow football with us. We waited for her dentures to pop onto the table during the games, as if it was part of the fun.

The refusal to divorce had a negative effect on us all. We all kept asking her to get rid of him, but she was adamant that she would not. I suppose it was even harder for his other children, the ones from his second family. When they needed proof of their parents' marriage, it was not available.

Many years later, I met my father's grandson, Paul. His mother was one of the six children dad had with Lily. He was a young man and told me I was the spitting image of his mother. He was traveling to Canada and had found my brother Alan in Niagara Falls, where he was performing.

Paul mentioned that if his grandparents had been married, the children might have emigrated more easily. I don't know if that was true or not, but it seemed like a rule at the time. I now realise I should have asked more about that other family, those half-siblings. I regret not learning more about them. Things are easier to track down now, and perhaps I could still find them.

I believe that my mother was wrong to cling so stubbornly to my father. Life might have been a little easier, a little more peaceful. I often wonder what happiness we might have found if she'd let go sooner.

Above all, I always wished for a father of my own. I envied the other children who had one, even if they weren't perfect. Having a father seemed to be a ticket to a better life, to getting on the waiting list for an affordable Council house. Mum tried to get us that, tried so many times, but it never worked. She was a single mother, and that made everything so much harder. I guess a father might have taken away one more reason I was bullied and made things a little easier to face.

CHAPTER 20

Exams and a New School

When I was 11, I took a test that might have got me into the Technical College, or the Tech as it was widely known, in Colchester, which was basically a high school. I didn't pass the first time, so I ended up at Brightlingsea Secondary School instead (BSS). When I was 13, I took the test again and passed.

We were taken to Brightlingsea every day by bus. The lessons at this school were different. I would miss the classes at Wivenhoe that taught me how to sew and knit, to dance, and sing folk songs. I was relieved to find out that Alan would also be at BSS. Knowing that he would be around at school made me feel more confident about facing the new environment.

I didn't know much about the school beforehand, only that there would be new faces and lessons awaiting me. However, after school began, I saw Alan less often. He was in the same class as me, but there were other new faces to get to know.

Soon, I noticed Tom, who became heartthrob #2. Tall and blonde. He liked me too, but there was competition from a younger girl, who was much cuter and better dressed, as her mother made all her clothes. She had dimples and big brown eyes. I now had two boys in my heart and there was to be more. It was quite innocent on my part, and we only ever exchanged kisses, not body fluids. It's a bit different these days when children are exposed to everything, including sex, drugs, and rock 'n' roll. We were shielded from most of it. It feels good to look back on this innocent time without regrets. I can't speak for the other girls, but I know I was chaste.

I spent two years at BSS. I was a shy kid who didn't speak up much, always feeling awkward and lonely. Sometimes I acted out in class and got a detention just to feel a part of the crowd. After getting a detention, I became friends with Angela and Pauline, and I was invited to a sleepover at Angela's house. That was a big deal for me.

But Mr. Palmer, the headmaster, was really strict. If you were given a detention, you also got caned on the hands and thankfully not on the backside, in his study. Contrary to what some might think today, it didn't mess me up psychologically. We just accepted it as part of the punishment.

Many kids went to summer camp every year, but I never got to go because I didn't have the money. The kids at BSS were way more unruly than I remembered at primary school. The age range was 13 to 16. It wasn't just the students who were bullied; the new teachers faced bullying too. Our class was very noisy and raucous, and the shy student teachers were drawn in, like magnets, to the madness.

I remember an incident involving a student teacher. She had a very large bust and a soft voice. The boys were fascinated by her bust. They constantly talked about 'tits' and gave this teacher unpleasant nicknames like Miss Knockers, Miss Big Boobs, and Miss Titmouse. Their bullying was relentless and unmerciful.

On this particular day, the teacher was not in the room, but the whole class was. One of the boys drew a huge pair of breasts on the blackboard with enormous nipples. Everyone found it hilarious, including the girls. I didn't take part, but I didn't say anything either, so I was just as guilty as everyone else.

When the young woman teacher walked into the room, she stared in shock at the drawing, while the class watched her reaction closely. She said nothing but turned beet red and burst into loud crying, sobbing her heart out at the unkindness of the class. She was utterly mortified and ran from the room straight to Mr. Palmer's office and reported us all. We were all quiet when Mr. Palmer walked in. He had his cane in his hand. We knew we had gone too far. He wiped the blackboard clean. Then he called us up to the front, one by one. He gave us all three of his best canings, on our hands, girls and boys alike, all equally guilty. We deserved it, and we never did anything like that again.

Teacher's Pet

I was assigned to D'Arcy House with Mr. Norton as the head of the House. He was my homeroom teacher, and my brother had been in his class before me. When he found out I was

Alan's sister, he had me sit right in front, directly under his nose. Before then, I had moved to the back of the room, where I could keep an eye on Alan and Tom. I thought they were pretty cute.

I never thought I was the teacher's pet, but the other children believed I was. I had no choice about where I sat. Mr. Norton was the English teacher. I excelled at English, spelling, writing, and composition; I loved all of it. He would often call on me to read aloud or provide the correct spelling. I discovered that my brother Alan was one of his favourite pupils, so that's why I was seated at the front. No passing notes under his eagle eyes. He was strict but fair, and I came to like him.

Mr. Norton was small in stature, but the children respected him. He was very straightforward and would walk along the aisles. If you appeared distracted, he would stop to ask a question or move you to a seat closer to him. He always seemed to notice when my mind drifted away from the lesson. He would call on me to read aloud. I usually kept reading while the others followed along with the lesson, so I was often caught. Then I would have to ask him where we were in the lesson. I think that was his idea of fun. He caught me several times. We were reading Prester John in class. I thought it was boring, but I liked the bits about the herds of animals – the wildebeest.

In addition to teaching English and Math, he was a soccer fanatic. He also taught soccer. The boys on the soccer team were looked on more favourably than those of us who didn't play. Since girls didn't play soccer then, we didn't have a hope in hell of being his favourite pet.

Tom was the teacher's favourite in class. He was a good soccer player, tall and blonde, although I doubt Mr. Norton was impressed by his looks. I was, though. A well-placed question from Tom could send Mr. Norton off in another direction, often about the popular professional soccer players of the day. The boys were devious in their attempts to distract him. I liked him, though. He had helped me on a couple of occasions, once when I was trapped in the library and another time when I had a fight with a girl in the yard.

On the day of the fight, I had wanted to play netball with the girls in the playground during the afternoon break. They wouldn't let me, so I decided to take the ball. I picked it up and ran with it. They chased me and hit me. I hit back but ended up with a black eye and a rip in my blouse. The whistle blew and we went back to class. When Mr. Norton saw me, he told me to stand up.

"What happened to you, Joy?" he asked. The class grew very silent, listening carefully.

"Please, sir, I had a fight," I said. There was a brief silence, then a titter, and soon laughter broke out all around.

"Did you want to take up boxing?" he asked.

"No, sir, thank you, sir," I replied, as I sat down.

The bubble burst! He had a smile on his face for the rest of the class, but he didn't call on me to do anything. He left me undisturbed, licking my wounds. I was grateful.

CHAPTER 21

Raging Hormones

During the two years I spent at BSS, it seemed like the boys had lost control and gone crazy. Any girl showing the slightest signs of breast development became a target. It made life so difficult for girls like me. Looking back on all the times sexual assault went unpunished, I realize how much has changed, and yet not enough.

It wasn't a good time for me. Between the tough times at home where we were struggling to get by and feeling targeted at school, I started to dread going there. The lucky girls had training bras, but for unlucky girls like me, that wasn't an option. My mother couldn't afford a bra for me, which only made things worse because I couldn't hide my shape anymore.

The boys didn't just stare at the front of our sweaters; they were always trying to slip their hands underneath to feel the prizes. It was a constant, unpleasant game of dodging their hands. If you resisted, one boy would hold your arms while the other tried to get a feel – it was clearly what would now be called sexual assault and harassment. Most of this went on in the classroom before the teacher arrived. The creepy boys had this primal instinct, a kind of animal-like mating frenzy. They knew what they wanted and would do anything to satisfy their desires.

Many of our lunch hours were spent avoiding the opposite sex. Things often got out of hand quickly. Sometimes the boys would pick on one girl, separating her from the rest of us. It reminded me of how wild animals target the weakest in the pack to chase down.

The boys would chase after us and then isolate the girl they chose. Usually, it was a smaller girl with a developing body who wasn't a great runner. The boys, many of whom played soccer and were much faster, would easily catch her and divert her into a secluded area. Once there, she'd panic and run the wrong way instead of towards the school and run into the woods. Then the boys caught her, pushed her down to the ground, pulled her dress up and inappropriately exposed her. Hands would grab at her, trying to feel where they shouldn't, making us all feel helpless and upset.

One time, a student teacher was strolling and caught the mob of boys and dispersed them. Sometimes, the girls weren't rescued. They'd be muddy and hysterical, and taken to the nurses' room to clean up. It still shocks me how this all happened so openly and that the boys were never punished. Their harassment escalated within the school.

One day, Mr. Norton, my homeroom teacher, asked me to be the class librarian. He liked me because he had taught my brother before me and felt a connection. As a class librarian, I had to be in the library when my classmates wanted to borrow a book. I'd write their names in a ledger, stamp their books, and then they could head back to class.

The library was a narrow room between two classrooms. It had a window at the opposite end of the door, with a balcony outside.

For the most part, I was able to do my job well and quickly. However, one day, three boys came in, not with books in mind, but for a touchy-feely session. Two of them approached the desk where I sat, reaching out to touch me. The third boy watched the door. I backed up and ran towards the window, which was open. I escaped onto the small balcony and started screaming.

As the boys kept coming closer, I climbed over the railing and held on. A teacher from the neighbouring classroom heard me and rushed in to help. I was rescued that time. I was hysterical and told everything to Mr. Norton, my teacher. The boys were given detention and received a caning. I decided to resign from my role as the class librarian.

On another day during our science class, the teacher had to leave the room. One of the boys grabbed me and tried to pull me to the back of the room. I held onto my desk while the boy grabbed my sweater sleeve. A couple of girls were also holding onto me. My left hand slipped into the sleeve, and it was pulled so hard that it ripped away from the bodice. The teacher returned, and that activity stopped. The school nurse sewed it up for me before I got on the bus home.

The boys started to get a bit smarter about their harassment and kept a lower profile. They found quieter spots to torment and assault girls, away from prying eyes. We were pulled into bushes while walking home from school, with underwear routinely torn, skirts muddied, and buttons ripped from blouses. On the surface, their pack mentality quietened. On the bus home from BSS, it was better to sit downstairs because upstairs could be dangerous, out of the driver's watchful eye. It was common knowledge that it was safer downstairs.

There was one girl at school who was quite promiscuous and fed into the sexual frenzy of that time. She was very open about what happened up there on the bus. She was the only girl on the top deck. When they surrounded her, she calmly lifted her sweater and showed them her breasts. Then she allowed each boy to touch them. They all got to satisfy their curiosity that day. She didn't mind at all and told us all about it at school the next day. She described how she lay down on the seat, lifted her skirt, pulled her pants down, and showed them her private parts. She was exploring her own curiosity as well as theirs. I was in shock and incredulous at her boldness.

She eventually allowed touching and more on the top deck. At least that is her account. She was a willing participant in the sexual games. She said she had been all the way, but not on the bus; only out in the fields and woods where we all played. She told us that at home, she would stand naked in front of her bedroom window and put on a show when the boys gathered in front of the house. She knew an awful lot about sex for someone my age. I was totally ignorant, but didn't mind listening to her daring adventures out of sheer curiosity.

When I was 13, I passed the exam to get into high school at Colchester Technical College, the Tech, which marked a huge turning point. We all wore uniforms at the Tech, so I didn't stand out anymore.

Life was easier then. The boys behaved better, and I finally got a bra.

When I turned 14, mum said she would go to the store, Curry's, to look at bikes for me.

She found a bike and paid a deposit, just like she did with the stove a few years back. She paid for it in installments. I went with her to pick up the bike. Since I didn't know how to ride a bike yet, we had to work out how to get it home. She let me choose the bike I liked in the shop. I picked a shiny black one with 3 gears, a bell, and racing stripes on the handlebars.

Mum said we could take the train home, so we walked the bike to the station with me on one side and mum on the other. When the train got to Wivenhoe, we walked home the same way. I didn't want to practice in front of anyone else.

I was so excited to finally get my own bike. I was still at the Tech then, so I guessed I could ride my bike to school. When we brought the bike home, I wheeled it up and down the lane. Eventually, I draped my foot across and straddled the bike. Holding on very carefully, I placed my right foot on the pedal, then stood up and did the same with my left foot, turning the pedals. I practised this for some time until I could pedal for a few minutes without stopping. I pedalled the bike back to our house. It was a start. I had to practice on the road next to it, or on the path through the churchyard. I did this regularly until I felt secure in my balance on the bike.

Quickly, I learned how to ride it and once I got the hang of it, I could keep up with the other kids when they rode around. Later, I rode the bike to work.

However, I never did learn how to start the bike with one foot on the pedal and then whip my body through to get my second foot on the moving pedal. I stuck to starting from a stationary position. It felt much safer for me. Still, I didn't quite feel like a real bike rider because of that.

My first ride was up the High street to Maggie's house. She had taken me along on her bike a few times, with me sitting on the back, but I wasn't sure I was ready to ride double. She brought her bike out, and we pedalled up the High street, around Bellevue road, to Rectory road, and then back home.

Getting a bike opened up a whole new world. After a few weeks, I was riding into Colchester with friends or on my own, riding around the village, or heading out to Brightlingsea, Elmstead, or Alresford. We'd cross the river Colne from Wivenhoe Quay on the ferry, holding our bikes upright, and then explore Fingringhoe. There was a gooseberry farm there, so we'd pick some and bring a few home.

There were many new places to explore on my shiny new bike. Down to the beaches along the river, to the quayside, and even to places I wasn't sure I could make it to, but I decided to try anyway, just to do what everyone else was doing, having a bit of fun.

Finally, there was one thing that made me feel like I truly belonged: I was finally a bona fide bike owner.

CHAPTER 22
The 'Tech' (1948-1952)

Mum and I went shopping for my bottle-green blazer, striped tie, matching skirt, and white blouse, which was the usual uniform for the Tech, short for the Technical College and School of Art. I was 13 and felt pretty special wearing what all the other girls wore. In the summer, our uniform switched to green gingham dresses. We could choose the style, buy the fabric, and make our own, or just pick one ready-made from the shop where we bought the uniform.

On my first day at the new school, I already had a strong feeling I was going to like it. Maggie had also made it into the Tech, so we took the bus together. I finally felt like I might belong and no longer carry the stigma of coming from a fatherless and impoverished home.

The bus dropped us off at the top of North Hill. We walked down to the Tech, passing lots of students all dressed the same. The boys wore grey trousers with green blazers.

When we got to the school, there was a general assembly. It was a chance to check out the boys. My eye caught a blonde boy with a lock of hair falling over his left eye – Peter Morris. I thought that he looked pretty cool. I also saw a tall, handsome boy with blonde hair named John Hart. I did end up dating John. I earnestly hoped these two might be in my class. Around that time, I also tucked Tom and Alan into a little corner of my heart, where they would stay for many years.

I was so happy that Maggie was in my class. She was a good friend, and we never fought or fell out over silly teenager stuff.

I felt more at home at The Tech and quickly made new friends. We hung out together, and during holidays, we'd all head down to Clacton by the seaside to meet up with the girls who lived there. We had a lot of good times.

This wasn't a troublemaker crowd; we all came from different backgrounds, but that didn't really matter. We all clicked pretty well – the girls from modest families and those from wealthier ones. Life at The Tech was so much better for me than it had been at BSS. The boys in my class were well-mannered and behaved better than the rowdy, hormonal boys back at BSS.

In the class photos, I am seated in the front row, with my big, bouncy, super cool curls. We're all in our summer clothes and some homemade dresses, but all in that green and white checked gingham. I loved wearing the school uniform, and I even made some of my own dresses. We didn't have a sewing machine, but those sewing instructions from Primary School came in handy for hand-sewing my dresses for high school. We got to pick our own patterns for summer dresses, and gathered skirts were all the rage back then.

Looking back now, with a petticoat underneath, it added a bit of weight to us and made us look a bit heavier. I considered myself a chunky girl back then. Those dresses didn't help, but I didn't realize that at the time. I just loved wearing what I wanted; my style of choice. My favourite school dress was a green gingham check with dropped shoulder seams, sleeveless, V-neck, and a gored skirt, paired with a wide belt. The collar often flopped open. I even knitted a green bolero, or what people now call a shrug that covered the shoulders to go over the dress.

I was way happier at The Tech than I ever was at BSS. Not every class was perfect, but I loved art and still do. I had a knack for it, and the teacher even said I had a natural talent. I was also a decent typist and did well with shorthand, even though I never really liked it. English and literature were my favourites; they made me read a lot, which I still do today. Math was a no-go; I was terrible at it, though I managed to do well in business arithmetic.

Before I started at The Tech, my mum paid for me to get a perm, so no more ragged ringlets! My hair used to curl all around my face and the idea was to hide my huge ears that stuck out.

I thought my ears were gigantic and ugly, and I hated them. I often dreamed of having flat ears, like little shells close to my head, instead of the big, wide-open ears like a taxi with the doors wide open. My brothers liked to tease me about them. Alan was the only one with nice, flat ears. He had inherited mum's tiny, flat ears, and that was the only thing about him that I admired. The other two brothers had ears like mine, but only worse. I guess dad's the one who gave us the big ears.

It took me a few years to overcome the ear phobia. For most of my youth, I kept them hidden away from view. I was pretty insecure in those days.

My other phobia was my teeth. When I was a kid, I'd wedge things between my front teeth, which eventually pushed them apart and left a lopsided V-shaped gap. I was so self-conscious about it, I hardly ever smiled or showed my teeth. Usually, I kept my mouth closed and my ears covered; it was a daily ritual.

When I turned 14, I finally got my two front teeth capped. It felt amazing to be able to show my teeth and smile openly again. That little change gave my confidence a big boost.

It was a happy time when those dropped-stitch bobbly scarves were all the rage. I knitted one myself and wrapped it around my tight curls and awkward ears. The weight of the bobbles over my shoulders kept it in place. That way of hiding my ugly ears had an unexpected perk: the boys could finally see my face! I could actually smile! They began to notice me and what they described as a sweet, angelic face after I pulled my hair back, with only my oval face in view.

As my curly, permed hair grew out, I used a simple black velvet headband to cover my ears. That little disguise, along with my growing bust, seemed to make them sit up even more and take notice. I was grateful that it wasn't the same kind of awful attention and harassment I used to get from the boys at BSS.

John, the blond guy in my class, noticed me. He seemed to like me, but I heard he had a girlfriend in Harwich, where he lived, so I didn't see much chance for us. Still, I enjoyed hanging out with him at school during recess and lunch, and I did manage to see him during school holidays when he came to

Wivenhoe. He chummed around with Colin and Miles, so the three of them, along with Maggie, me and the other girls, spent happy and innocent times, flirting in the school fields.

Another big part of my life at that time was related to my periods, which I had since I was nine. I really wished I had some sanitary towels at home, but mum just couldn't afford them, so I'd get mine from the school nurse. They were part of that free package they handed out. Before sanitary towels, girls my age had to use a folded cloth, kind of like a tea towel, with loops that hooked onto a belt around the waist. I guess that's what my mum had to wear back then. The cloth was washed and used again between periods.

Thank goodness for school nurses, who always had proper sanitary towels available for girls like me who couldn't afford them. We called our periods 'the curse' or 'time of the month,' and oddly, the girls around me celebrated having period pains because it meant we were growing up. It felt like a rite of passage and made us feel more grown-up. Most of us didn't even realise that we could get pregnant after getting our period.

Things have changed a lot since those days. Life was different, and girls were less likely to be promiscuous or at least, most of them.

I enjoyed my time at The Tech. I got good marks for most things, especially English subjects, art, which I was good at, business arithmetic, typing and shorthand. French wasn't my strong suit, and the teacher wasn't very patient with those of us who didn't pick up the language quickly. When a French girl arrived at the school, conversation flowed between the teacher and the student, and we learned nothing. Eventually, she refused to teach our class, so we escaped her.

I left The Tech when I was 16. The art teacher suggested I go to Art college, but I told him we couldn't afford it. So, I headed into the secretarial world. Nursing was another option, but I knew I wouldn't be good at it as I get easily queasy by blood. Too many things could turn my stomach.

Before leaving school, we were supposed to apply for jobs, and I did. I got a position at Edmunds Walker, an auto supply company. On our last day, we took photos and we were allowed to wear the clothes we'd start our new jobs in. I wore a white swing jacket, a black pencil skirt, black high heels, and had a black band around my fairly long hair.

Joy on her final day at the Tech in 1952.

My time at the Tech lasted three years and passed quickly. It felt like no time at all since we first started. It was strange to think we'd now be working women. I hoped I'd like it, though I was still pretty shy. Having Maggie as a friend gave me a bit of confidence, and I was hoping her confidence would rub off on me. She'd be working pretty close to me, at a company over in the Hythe area of Colchester.

The relationships with the boys at the Tech were actually pleasant. We actually talked to each other, no more frantic grabbing in class. After I pushed my hair back from my face, I'd get compliments about my eyes. I was 14 and looked in the mirror at my crooked teeth, promising myself I'd get them fixed with crowns, and I did. I loved having those crowns; they let me smile without feeling self-conscious.

Due to the diets we were on at the time, my skin used to break out in pimples. I had no clue how to clear up my skin. My dear friend Maggie had a lovely complexion, beautiful teeth, and manageable hair kept in a sleek bob. She was outgoing and friendly, and the boys liked her. She could sail and swim. I was afraid of the water.

I remember when we were both 12. I fell off the quay at Wivenhoe among the boats. Maggie jumped in to save me. She could swim well, but I panicked and grabbed her, holding her underwater. Luckily, a sailor nearby jumped in and rescued us both. Mum was called while I was still on the ground. She took me home, and I was fine. Still, I was traumatized by the near-death experience and was aware that there had been a few drownings in the River Colne while I was growing up there.

Maggie had regular holidays with her family. The year before I left school, mum took us down to Devon to a holiday camp. That was our first holiday. We went with Ian and his fiancée Babs, her parents, Mr. and Mrs. Reynolds, and Alan, my brother. We had a great time. Mum entered me in a singing competition. I sang "I Talk to the Trees," which wasn't my first choice. I wanted to sing "Blue Moon," but someone else grabbed it.

There was a boy named Derek in the chorus, and he fancied me. He had acne, and I didn't fancy him at all. When the holiday finished and we headed to the train station, he asked to stay in touch. I didn't have a phone, so I gave him Maggie's number, which was actually the police phone number, which was a bit naughty. When I told her, she just laughed. When he called, I told him not to call me any more because I wasn't interested. We both had a laugh when I hung up. That was that.

Bye-bye, Derek!

CHAPTER 23

Working Girl and Losing Maggie

Back in 1952, I landed my first job. I'd usually hop on the bus from Wivenhoe to the Hythe, then walk or bike to the office. I was working upstairs and quickly learned I was the one responsible for making the tea. My boss was right next door, and a seasoned female coworker who had been there for years kindly showed me the ropes. She was the only other woman in the office. That job was the start of a meaningful professional journey.

On my first day, I carefully brought the tea downstairs in high heels and balanced the cups on the tray. The next day, my heel caught on a stair and I tumbled down. The cups broke and the hot tea spilled everywhere. I felt beaten up and very embarrassed to have fallen. I was feeling so clever about managing it the first day. After that accident, an arrangement was made to have the staff come upstairs for their tea.

My boss wasn't paying me much, and after a couple of weeks, I finally had the nerve to ask for a raise. He had started me at 15 shillings and agreed to bump it up to 17 shillings and sixpence. Since one pound is roughly two Canadian dollars, I'll let you do the math. One of the employees asked me to go get his cigarettes. I did it once, but then told him I wouldn't do it again, because I wasn't being paid to do that.

I had only been there a couple of weeks when Maggie told me her dad had been transferred to Romford, so she'd be moving soon. When she knew the date, she gave her notice at work. Her company threw her a going-away party. She was my first best friend, and I knew I'd miss her a lot.

Maggie and her family moved to Romford. I spent a weekend with her soon after they moved into their new house. Maggie told me about a cute boy next door named Dennis. I didn't get to meet him because he was away at the time. We had a really nice weekend together, and then I caught the train back to Wivenhoe.

A few days later, I heard that Maggie had been killed. She had gone for a walk with Dennis, and while they were walking at Gallows Corners, a car that was traveling too fast had hit them. They both died instantly. Maggie's dad was on duty and was called to the scene. It was just devastating. The service was held in Wivenhoe. I wore black and went to say goodbye to my beautiful best friend, Maggie. It was a long, painful time before I found another close friend. Rest in peace, Maggie.

A photo of Joy's best friend, Maggie, and a newspaper article about Maggie's tragic death in 1953.

Life went on at work. My original boss left, and a new one showed up, bringing along an adorable poodle puppy that I took care of during the day. It felt like a little bonus, but I was still missing Sandy, my brother Colin's golden retriever. I remember saying how much I'd love a dog like that. My new boss mentioned he needed to find a home for the puppy, and I begged to take him. He saw how I cared for this puppy and knew I'd be good to him. I brought him home that very day and named him Nicki. I took him to work with me until he was big enough to stay on his own. We went on lots of walks around the village, and I loved him to bits. I stayed at that job for a couple of years.

Joy's dog Nicki in 1953.

Nicki in Joy's family's garden in 1953.

Joy at work in 1955.

Joy in the village, 1955.

We had been discussing as a family about moving to another country to escape the poverty that still followed us. I knew I'd need to earn a bit more money to save for the travel fare. When I heard about a job at The Colchester Lathe Company paying around seven pounds a week, I decided it was time to make a move.

I applied and got the job of Senior Secretary. I was surprised to land it. I worked hard in the shipping and sales departments, and I was pretty good at writing letters. I hadn't learned to like shorthand, but when I couldn't understand what had been dictated, I could write something acceptable, and I don't believe the managers would remember exactly what they had said. Eventually, I was asked to write letters and just drop them for a signature. I liked that much better.

I became friends with quite a few of the girls at work. That's where I met Joyce Munson, who became a very good friend. She had a cute little car. When she gave me a ride, the door would fly open as we went around a corner, so I'd have to hold it closed. Eventually, Joyce married Arthur, and I was a bridesmaid at her wedding. Tragically, her first child, Philip, died suddenly in his sleep.

Sylvia was another good friend from work and we used to spend weekends cycling to the river to catch some sun. At the Lathe Company, we had to wear blue coveralls, which felt a bit like school uniforms. After I suffered from a bad sunburn, I was relieved that the coveralls covered my bright red skin. Sylvia was a beautiful girl and had married her boyfriend. She had a lovely baby boy, but sadly, she suffered from postpartum depression and took her own life by hanging herself while she was getting treatment.

Most of the time, I enjoyed my job at the Lathe Company and we worked from 8 am until 6 pm. But there was one very distressing incident. One evening, when we finished work at six and I was waiting for the bus outside, the chauffeur to the CEO pulled up and asked if I wanted a ride to Wivenhoe.

I said, 'Yes, thank you.' I knew him around the office, so he wasn't a stranger. He took me part of the way home, and suddenly pulled off into a field. He grabbed me and tried to kiss me. I punched him, got out of the car, and ran away. I was livid and walked all the way home.

The next day at work, he was hanging around, joking with the guys that he had hooked up with me in the car. I denied it, of course, but it was his word against mine. I had already told my boss what happened, hoping he'd get fired. But to my horror, he was still working there when I left for Canada in 1958.

This was a major turning point, and I learned the importance of trusting my instincts and standing up for myself, even when it's difficult.

CHAPTER 24

Saturday Night Dances

I looked forward to Saturday nights with a real sense of excitement. There was always a dance to attend. Most of the village teenagers went to the dances. We were usually taken in Mr. Peck's private coach. It was mostly used for adult day trips, but on Saturday nights, it was ours.

The coach waited for us at the top of the High Street, outside of Mr. Peck's garage. When it was full, we set off to wherever the dance was being held. The coach itself was one of his older models, with some of the seats a little worn. We didn't mind. We sat in our perfume bubble, focusing on getting to the dance and hoping we wouldn't be wallflowers.

Getting ready for these dances took some time. The girls in the village would put on heavy makeup, emphasizing bold eyes outlined with dark eyebrows drawn in with a pencil, and eyelids painted to match their dresses. They'd also put on foundation, powder, and rouge on their cheeks. The final touch was usually bright red lipstick.

This level of preparation took quite a while. Most of the time, we had to do it outside the house because most parents back then would say, "Wash that off" or something similar. So we would apply the makeup outdoors and wipe it off before heading back home. We all thought we looked pretty special, but we probably looked like little tarts. We just wanted to seem older or be older. We would spray on a lot of perfume. Back then, we didn't know about allergic reactions. We smelled fantastic, with waves of heavy fragrance drifting off our glamorous bodies.

The band at the hall we went to was made up of local lads, all amateur musicians who united to form a band. Most villages had one like it. We paid about a dime to get into the hall.

My girlfriends and I wondered if anyone would ask us to dance. Hope filled my heart that when a boy crossed the hall, he would ask me. Sometimes they asked me, sometimes they did not. It was customary for the boys to sit on one side of the hall and the girls on the other. The floor was left for dancing.

It was fun sitting and watching the boys to see who danced better. The best dancers were the ones we hoped to be asked by; otherwise, you might end up accidentally stepping on toes during the dance. As we sat and observed the boys, they watched us in return. We waited to be asked. At that time, I had never heard of ladies' choice dances. Even if such dances had existed, I doubt most of us would have been brave enough to ask a boy to dance. Well, I'll never know the answer to that. But later in life, I did ask quite a few boys to dance.

Girls started dancing together because there were no partners available. In those days, I was around 15 but felt more like 20. I spent my time waiting for someone to ask me to dance. There was no alcohol at these dances, so we simply sipped lemonade. On the floor, several couples danced. The boys swung the girls around as best as they could, while the girls' skirts swished as they turned and twirled during lively dances. I loved the dresses of that era, with their flared, full skirts that made dancing so much fun.

It was simple but exciting. Dancing in village halls during those days instilled in me a lifelong love of dancing. We were all fairly skilled at ballroom dancing because we had all taken lessons. Most of the young people in the villages at that time attended lessons. I can also trace my love of performing back to those impromptu concerts at home.

When we climbed onto the bus to head home, we would compare notes about our experiences. It was at one of these dances, when I was 16, where I met my future fiancé.

Those years were happy times, going to Saturday night dances in Wivenhoe and other nearby villages. In retrospect, those moments of innocence and joy shaped my understanding of life: that growing up is a dance of its own, full of unexpected twists and turns, where the beauty of shared experiences and awkward moments co-exist and flow together.

CHAPTER 25

Pawning the Ring

I had known John for quite a while, mostly as a friend around the village and also on the bus to school and work in Colchester. His parents ran a shop in Wivenhoe, and he went to the Boys High School in Colchester. I always thought he was kind of a smartass and liked to be sarcastic. He often called people 'Mush,' which I found to be common slang but also a bit rude.

Once I snapped back, telling him, "MY NAME IS JOY!" because I felt he was being disrespectful. I guess I might be a bit of a name snob myself – I feel the same about casually saying, "Hey, you." I never thought I'd hear from him again, but it turned out he respected me for having some standards. After that, he always used my name.

One night at a Saturday dance, John asked me to dance. He hadn't done that before, so I was surprised but said yes. He never said anything about my new perfect teeth after I had a dental procedure, and I liked him for that. We talked about everything under the sun, and he kept asking me to dance. He was tall, a couple of years older than me, and a good dancer. He wasn't exactly handsome in the usual way, but he had a presence about him.

He told me he had always liked me but was too shy to ask me out. After dancing and talking with him, I started to like him. He was pretty funny, with a good sense of humour. His sarcasm was probably just shyness and a lack of confidence when talking to girls. I told him I'd go out with him, but only if he stopped calling me stupid names. He apologized and said he wouldn't do it again. A lot of boys did that when they didn't know how to approach a girl, like pulling pigtails to get attention.

After we danced all night at the village dance, we sat together on the bus and kissed all the way home. He was a good kisser and I enjoyed it. That's how we started dating. We went to dances, movies, took walks, and grabbed drinks together. He was very sexy and always horny. We saw each other almost every day and always found a quiet spot to cuddle. I was afraid of getting pregnant, which would have been a huge disgrace at the time, so we didn't go all the way.

It was a very exciting, sensual time. We would have eventually moved on to the real thing. Seeing him on the bus and exchanging smiles was thrilling. Our connection was extremely intense, and I could tell he often had an erection and was constantly fantasising about me. We were mad about each other.

Then he was called up for National Service and joined the Royal Air Force when he turned 18 and had to report to

Wattisham near Ipswich. We had been dating for a couple of years by then.

While he was in the RAF, he wrote to me every day, sending me very sexy, descriptive letters. I would wait each day for the postman to arrive and then read the letters on the bus on my way into work. The bus rides got pretty steamy. John's sexy letters kept coming during his two years in the Air Force. He often imagined different scenarios where we would be making mind-blowing love.

When he came home, we had a joyful reunion. He needed to look for a job, and follow in his father's footsteps in insurance. His parents had moved to Blackheath in London, and John was searching for work there. They had a nice flat there, and I visited on some weekends. John had a brother and a sister, both younger than him. His Granny also lived in the flat with them.

I liked his dad. He was a quiet man, but really kind to me. I think he could tell I felt out of my depth staying in that fancy flat when I was used to living in a dump. Honestly, I did feel uncomfortable staying with them.

With John now working in London and me still in Wivenhoe, we often talked about getting married. Neither of us liked the distance between us. One weekend around my birthday in 1955, John asked me to marry him. He gave me a beautiful ring, a family heirloom that had belonged to his grandmother. We made plans to get married the following spring of 1956. I was working at the Lathe Company at the time, and I loved showing off this stunning ring to my coworkers. Planning our wedding, which was going to be in Wivenhoe, was very exciting. I kept staring at the ring all day long and loved the way it sparkled in the sunlight as it sat on my finger.

Sometimes I went to London on weekends to see John. The only thing I didn't like was how little privacy we had in his apartment. We were never alone. I also didn't like the way his mother made Yorkshire pudding. It was very sloppy and served before the main meal. I struggled to eat it. Yorkshire pudding is usually crisp and rises out of the pan with mountains and valleys, but hers was flat and half-cooked, like a soggy pudding-cake hybrid that wasn't quite ready to come out of the oven.

John enjoyed his job in London. Around this time, I heard that his dad had been sent to prison for embezzlement. It made me sad. He was a very nice, gentle man.

Christmas was coming. John wouldn't be visiting me because he had an office party to go to.

I didn't know it then, but I wouldn't see him again for 22 years.

In January 1956, I received my first letter from John. It was a very different tone. It was a classic Dear John letter, but instead of Dear John, it was Dear Joy.

I was devastated to read that he had met someone at his office party and fallen in love with her. He asked for the ring to be returned to him.

To say I was heartbroken is putting it mildly. I cried all the time, both at work and at home. Everywhere I went, the word 'jilted' was being whispered around me. It affected my family so deeply that my mum reached out to a friend who had moved to Buckinghamshire, asking if I could take a holiday to get away from our village and the constant reminders of my lost love. John never returned to the village, so I never saw him again before we left in 1958.

I still had the ring and hadn't decided what to do about it. I figured that he wanted it back because it was a family heirloom. From what I understood, if a girl broke up with a boy, she returned the ring, but if the boy broke up with her, she kept it. I believe that rule still applies.

So, I headed over to Bucks County. It was quiet and peaceful there. But the husband took a fancy to me and ended up taking a bunch of photos of me on his bike, smoking a cigarette, sitting on his car. I didn't think much of it at the time; I thought he was just being nice. His wife, though, didn't see it that way. I wasn't interested in him at all. I decided to leave early. This short trip gave me time to think about my break-up, and I grew angrier with John for sleeping with a colleague. I was certain I would keep the ring.

When I got home, I wrote to John and told him I planned to keep the ring since he had broken off the engagement. I imagine his family wasn't too happy about that. My brother Alan was also working in London, and I asked him to find out what I might get if I sold the ring. He came back with a price that, at the time, seemed pretty generous. So I pawned it and decided to use the money for a holiday.

I went to a travel agent and inquired about Italy. I booked two weeks in Rapallo on the Italian Riviera for the summer. It was something to look forward to. I went back to work and planned time off for the trip. Apart from a holiday in Devon when I was 16, I hadn't been anywhere else except London. It felt like an adventure to look forward to.

A few local boys asked me out, and I went out with them and had friendly relationships. I didn't want to get serious with anyone at this point. I was still pretty heartbroken that after four years, John could break off our engagement through a cold letter.

Later, around 22 years later, I was in England and ran into John in a pub. I said to him, "Sorry about the ring," and he just shrugged. His marriage hadn't worked out. They divorced, and he remarried. I later heard he died at fifty. A friend sent me the obituary. I was saddened by the news. Somewhere, I believe his memoir is around. I wonder if I was in it. He's definitely in mine.

CHAPTER 26

The Trip that Changed My Life

I often find myself pondering what gave me the audacity to venture so far away to Italy. As a young girl, my world was small, confined to that tiny village where everyone knew everyone else. The only real break from the familiar was our brief holiday in Devon, England, which was a rare escape that marked my first steps beyond the fields and faces I had always known.

Yet, even with such limited experience, I carried within me a dream of distant foreign lands and new horizons. Listening to my mother recount her adventures abroad, her stories ignited a growing sense of curiosity and longing within me to explore the world.

I remember so clearly the day my brother Alan returned from his trip to Italy. His words about its beauty were riveting and stirred a deep longing that I could not shake. He had brought back a small, heart-shaped pair of earrings with amber stones, treasures that I still cherish and wear today. They remind me of that ache that accompanies a longing to see the world beyond my then small, mundane existence.

For a long time, I had repeatedly tried to rally friends and family for adventures of my own, hoping to find companionship to explore new countries. But each time, they backed out, leaving me to cancel plans and forfeit deposits. That repeated disappointment quietly turned into a resolve that if I could muster the courage to travel alone to Italy, perhaps I could face anything life might throw at me.

If Maggie had been alive then, I have no doubt she would have joined me on this trip to Italy in August 1956. I was twenty and would be turning twenty-one in October. As August drew nearer and my departure date approached, I felt a strange mix of excitement and apprehension flood over me. I was to travel alone to London, then down to Dover to board a ferry crossing to France, long before the Channel Tunnel made such journeys commonplace.

I remember applying for my first passport and holding that small rectangular document with my photograph for the first time; I could hardly contain my excitement. To this day, I preserve it along with the subsequent passports in the years that followed, each one a record of a young woman slowly finding her way.

On the boat, I met Ruth and Audrey, a couple of girls from Yorkshire, also bound for Rapallo, Italy, and both of them were staying at the same hotel as me. I was dressed in checkered capri pants and a short white faux-fur jacket; these clothes made me feel fashionable and carefree. I had packed a new swimsuit, eager to soak up the sun and get a tan while I was away.

My wardrobe consisted of a few lovely dresses given to me by my sister-in-law. These were gifts that either fell off a lorry or came straight from a dressmaker's samples. My brother Colin worked at a dress manufacturing place and often came home with garments strapped to his scooter and often had strange yet intriguing finds. His wife had a huge wardrobe filled with clothes, many still with tags attached. When I visited them before my trip, she told me to pick what I liked, so I did. A yellow pleated dress, a pale green floral silk dress, a pink sailor-style pleated skirt with a matching top, and a pink polka-dot dress. One was a red calf-length dress with buttons and a black belt. Perhaps these gorgeous dresses were stolen or perhaps not, but to me, they were simply beautiful. I had a love affair with fashion.

During this trip, I spent more time with Ruth and Audrey, the two girls I met on the boat. Together, we travelled through France and Switzerland by train, sharing stories and dreams while gazing out at landscapes that seemed straight out of a travel magazine. When we finally arrived in Rapallo and checked into our hotel, I was walking on cloud nine.

I wish I could remember whether I paid a single supplement. I probably did, although at the time I wouldn't have noticed, nor was I aware of the extra charge that singles had to pay for a room meant for two people. The travel agent had made all the arrangements for me, and I was so naïve then that I probably paid with no questions asked.

Little did I know then that those days would be some of the most formative of my life, forever shaping my understanding of independence, courage, and love. After we had unpacked our belongings, we gathered in a nearby restaurant for a meal. The waiters were cheeky and sweet, and I enjoyed their playful banter. We were exhausted from travel, so we arranged to meet for a dance after dinner once we had all taken a short nap.

I remember feeling so tired that I slept far longer than I had intended. When I finally woke, I put on the pale green silk floral dress I had brought, complete with dangling earrings and my sandals. I threw a lightweight shawl around my shoulders. Then I set out to find my new friends, full of anticipation. When I knocked on their door, there was no answer. My first thought was that they had gone out, perhaps because I had overslept. So I decided to look for them.

I walked out of the hotel and had to pass by a group of waiters standing outside. One of them, a young man who had served us earlier, suddenly came after me and yanked at my earring. Luckily, it was a clip-on, so it didn't hurt, but the incident left me feeling embarrassed yet curious about his actions. He was a bloke trying to get my attention in a strange way – something I had come across before in England! Some things are universal, no matter where you go.

I slipped away from their curious stares and followed the music I heard nearby, a melody that felt both familiar and tantalizing. It led me to a dance hall that was built just over the water. When I stepped inside, I was immediately aware of the vibrant energy filling the room. The song playing was Volare; its lively tune made my feet and arms pulse. I wanted to break out into a dance.

As I went inside to look around for my friends, I quickly realized they were not there. Instead, I felt shy to find so many pairs of brown eyes fixed upon me, their gazes intense. That moment was electric. I spoke no Italian except for a few words I had learned, and the language barrier made me feel vulnerable. I wasn't sure what to do next.

Then, almost as if by magic, a gentle hand guided me to a table, a soft drink was placed before me, and suddenly a line of eager dancers formed around the room, all wanting to dance with me. To my utter shock, I was the belle of the ball, so to speak, like something straight out of a Disney film!

That evening was nothing short of magical. I kept dancing with the next boy in line, each one handsome in a way I had never seen before. I had never met an Italian man before, and I was very mesmerised by their dark eyes and the way they moved with such passion. Italy, for me, was a place both strange and incredibly beautiful.

That night opened my eyes to new experiences, a taste of freedom and happiness I wouldn't forget for the rest of my life. I noticed that one young man was dancing with me more than anyone else. He told me in broken English that he would take me home after the dance and shooed away the other boys with a shy smile. He introduced himself as Luigi. He was strikingly handsome with luminous brown eyes with a glint of mischief, full lips that seemed almost to smile on their own, black hair hanging just over one eye, giving him an air of both mystery and charm. Despite his politeness and gentle spirit, I sensed a fiery strength within him.

After the dance, he led me down the hill to the hotel, kissed my hand tenderly, and said he would show me the famous Riviera the next morning. He planned to pick me up on his scooter, and I imagined what it would be like to ride on the cobblestones sitting behind him. I felt a deep sense of wonder that first evening in Italy, and floated up the stairs to bed, feeling in awe of the Cinderella-like time I had.

As I lay there in bed, I giggled when I realized that I was not thinking of the heartbreak I left behind or the man I had lost, John, but I was enthralled by a tall, dark stranger who had so unexpectedly entered my world. That night, I learned that sometimes, the most profound cures come unexpectedly, from the kindness of strangers, from new beginnings, and from a willingness to embrace the unknown. The pain from a broken heart seemed to fade for a moment, replaced by new desires stirring.

That morning, I sat with Ruth and Audrey over breakfast, telling them every detail about the night before. The waiter who served us was the very same man who had sneaked his hand into my ear the evening before and pinched my earring. I watched him set out rolls and coffee, his face unchanging. When I opened my roll, sure enough, my earring was inside. It struck me as a clever and sneaky little trick. And just then, Luigi walked in. He had his scooter parked outside the hotel, ready to take me on our little adventure. He had come to claim me for the morning. We agreed to meet the girls at the lido after lunch so I could introduce them to his friends.

His scooter was waiting outside in the warm sunlight. I was wearing the yellow dress I had brought, and Luigi looked at me and said, "You look like sunshine."

I suppose he meant I brought some brightness into his day. I distinctly recall feeling a little shy about it. I climbed onto the scooter and sat behind him very carefully, holding onto his waist tightly. It was a new kind of excitement. I had been on the back of a regular motorcycle before, but this was the first time on a scooter. It felt like we were flying as we sped down the roads with my hair flowing in the wind. That was before helmets were mandatory, and I remember feeling so alive, almost like I was discovering parts of myself I hadn't known before.

Everything around me was spectacularly beautiful and vibrant. The scenery was breathtaking, and I wanted to remember the details forever. I had this intense feeling that I was in a fairy tale, breathing it all in with a sense of freedom that came with being young with no responsibilities, dressed in my pretty yellow dress, riding behind Luigi.

He took me to the slopes above Rapallo, where the hills rolled gently and the sea sparkled below. When we reached Montallegro, Luigi parked the scooter, and we took a funicular railway up to the mountain's summit. At the top stood the Santuario di Montallegro, a stunning 16th-century church that houses a Byzantine icon believed to have miraculous powers. We didn't go inside because I wasn't dressed properly, but I felt the weight of history and faith in the air. We spent some time looking around, taking in the views, and then descended the mountain on the funicular railway.

Back on the scooter, Luigi drove me to a cozy little restaurant in Rapallo. That's where I had my very first pizza. It was the most wonderful thing I had ever tasted, and I learned about unisex toilets, which were a pit in a field behind the restaurant. I declined to use it, afraid I might fall in.

Rapallo was a place filled with amazing stories. It was where the movie The Barefoot Contessa had been filmed, which to my young eyes made it seem glamorous and mysterious. It also carried heavy history, for after the war, two treaties had been signed there. One treaty was between Italy and Yugoslavia and the other between the Germans and the Russians. I learned these details later. The esplanade with its old 16th century castle jutting into the sea was a reminder of times gone by and the enduring strength of a place that had seen much change.

In those heady days as a first-time traveller, I learned to appreciate more deeply the beauty around me and in people. I suppose that's what keeps me going still, holding onto those memories, understanding that there is something worth holding onto and learning from in times of setbacks.

After lunch, we made our way to the lido where I met Charlie, his friend who was traveling with him, and a couple of other boys. My two friends were also there. We swam in the water, though I didn't swim myself; I just enjoyed floating and feeling the coolness lap against my skin. We played and relaxed in the sun, and Luigi stayed by my side, quiet but watchful.

Later, we strolled along the esplanade, peering into shops. I bought a pair of micro red shorts, a raffia purse, and some wooden slide-on clogs. I still remember how daring that felt. I didn't know if I'd ever come back to Italy after we emigrated to Canada, so I thought I should look the part while I was there. I even got a haircut, an Italian style, with Luigi translating every word to the hairdresser. He took many black and white photos, capturing the simple moments that now seem so very precious.

Our days followed this pattern for the whole time I stayed in Rapallo. Luigi would pick me up each morning and take me to a different spot along the Riviera. One day, we went to Milan. I remember standing outside the magnificent Gothic Duomo, feeding pigeons and feeling disappointed that I hadn't packed a skirt or dress. I was wearing pants that day and women wearing trousers were not allowed to enter the Duomo. It was strictly prohibited. I wish I'd brought a scarf, too, but I hadn't checked the local customs and rules before traveling to Italy.

Milan was unspeakably stunning: the grandeur of the city, the taste of beauty everywhere I looked. We visited Castle Sforzesco; it looked plain from the outside, but inside I marvelled at Michelangelo's Rondanini Pieta, an unfinished sculpture of a dying Christ with his mother, the Virgin Mary, which is an exploration of death and salvation. It seemed so raw and sad.

What struck me most was the Galleria Vittorio Emanuele II. The marble floors, the glass dome, the intricate ironwork of Italy's oldest four-storey shopping arcade and a major landmark in Milan. It was like walking into a dream. I remember feeling a deep longing then, a desire to wear expensive designer clothes like Valentino, Gucci, Versace. These names meant nothing to me at the time, but I could sense the allure and prestige. I doubted I'd ever afford such things, but I held onto a dream that someday, I would be wearing designer clothes and jewellery. That visit to Milan made me realize how much I loved fashion, how it could give a person a sense of identity and pride.

We also visited La Scala that day. The grandeur of the historic opera house took my breath away. It opened in 1778 and can seat 1,800 people. Most of Italy's greatest opera singers have performed there and it is regarded as one of the leading opera and ballet theatres in the world. I felt grateful to have Luigi as my guide, someone kind and gentle who shared these wonders with me. Looking back now, I see how those days of exploration planted seeds of hope inside me. This exposure to rich historical sites inspired me to dream big and this has stayed with me through all the hard years that followed.

We spent countless days wandering through Genoa and Turin, then moving along to Portofino, Santa Margherita, Camogli, Zoagli, and Sestri Levante. The afternoons there were spent lounging on sun-warmed beaches and plunging into the cool water, a simple pleasure that seemed to make the world slow down for a while. In the evenings, we would gather together, sharing quiet moments and gentle and affectionate goodbyes as the sun dipped below the horizon.

I remember giving Luigi a photograph of myself that I had taken at work, an ordinary picture made special because he treasured it. Luigi was a talented photographer, and throughout the holiday, he captured many beautiful black-and-white images of the landscapes and of us, those little scenes that now feel like fragments of a dream.

When the trip came to an end, we said a loving goodbye and parted with tears and promises. He assured me that he would come to England the next year. On my twenty-first birthday in October 1956, I received a telegram from Luigi, in which he wished me a happy birthday and a delicate watercolour portrait he had commissioned in my honour. That painting still hangs on my wall today, a wonderful reminder of our innocent romance. Along with it came romantic messages in sweet broken English on the back of photos we had taken together. Each message was filled with a love that felt so real.

Joy and Luigi during her trip to Italy in 1956.

Joy in Camogli, Italy in 1956.

A watercolour painting that Luigi commissioned and mailed to Joy as a birthday gift in 1956.

Studio photos of Joy taken before her trip to Italy in 1956. Luigi used these photos to commission a watercolour painting of Joy (see the painting above).

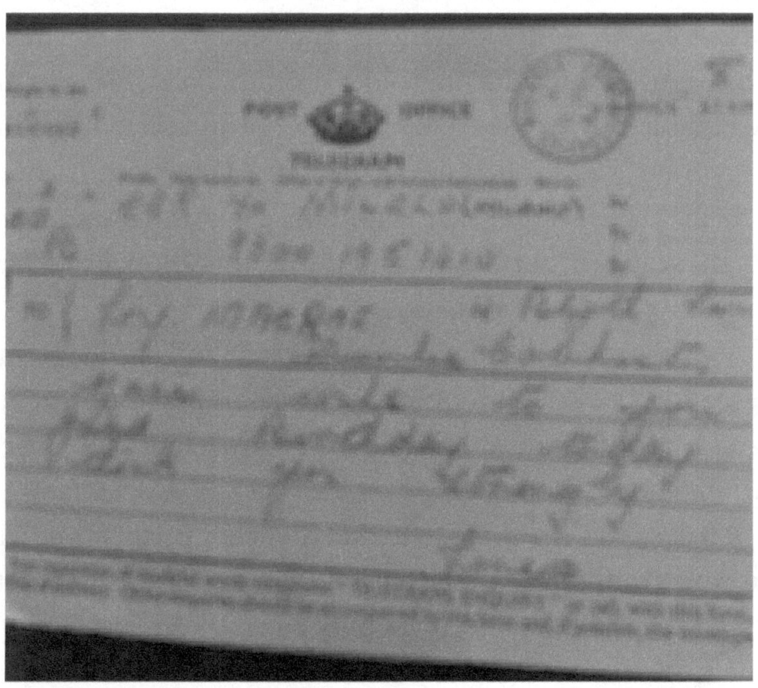

A telegram that Luigi sent to Joy on her birthday in 1956.

At Christmas, he sent me another gift, this time a Panettone cake, the traditional Italian Christmas cake. Its sweet, rich aroma filled our home. We kept up our correspondence, writing back and forth as the months passed. Then came the day Luigi came to England. He first went to Paris for a few days, and then he traveled to London. I met him in Colchester, and from there we took the train down to Wivenhoe, my childhood town. Luigi was able to stay in the boys' room because Ian and Alan had already emigrated to Canada. Ian had moved to Hamilton, Ontario, with his wife Barb, and Alan had settled in Vancouver, British Columbia.

My mother and I had plans to follow the boys in 1958. Alan's fiancée was coming with us. During Luigi's visit, I showed him around London and the countryside near Wivenhoe. It was a lovely holiday, even if I knew deep down that we were not meant to be together. Luigi met my older brother Colin, his wife, and their children when we were in London, and I introduced him to my friends and colleagues at the Lathe Company. A couple of them seemed quite taken with him. He was handsome in a way that caught your breath, and my mother thought he was a lovely boy. I knew he was, too.

We rode trains through the countryside and headed toward the seaside. But I never took him to the churches nearby, a small regret I carry even now. I should have shown him those places, but somehow I didn't.

That was the first time I had ever spent any quality time with someone from the Catholic faith. Luigi was raised in a stricter church than I knew, and I was only an Anglican girl who had gone to church and Sunday school during my childhood. As

I grew older, I drifted away from my faith, but Luigi took me to places of worship that mattered to him. I learned that his father had been part of the resistance during the war, had been captured and executed in front of his mother and brother. That piece of his story told me there was trauma in his life that I could not fully understand.

Given my mother's strength and resilience during the war, I never had the heart to tell her that I had fallen for an Italian boy when I was supposed to go to Canada. My heart told me I loved Luigi, but my mind knew it couldn't be. Our backgrounds, our religions, and what my family planned for our future all seemed to stand in the way.

Telling my mother I was not going to Canada would have been unthinkable after I spent three years working and sacrificing to save for our move, knowing she depended on me, knowing how she had carried us through all the hardships as a single mother. It simply wasn't in my nature or in my DNA to cause her worry or pain. Sometimes love means knowing when to let go, even if your heart is breaking.

I still remember that trip to Italy as if it were yesterday, with vivid, almost raw detail. I was only twenty then; now I'm ninety, yet that experience remains a sacred and unchangeable part of me. There was something extraordinary about Italy, an ineffable quality that I cannot quite explain but have always yearned for. I still miss that feeling deeply. But life moves on.

If Luigi and I had been lovers, maybe I wouldn't have been as strong. I knew he loved me, and I loved him in return. We had a pure connection, but love itself was not enough.

If I could go back in time, I might have chosen differently, but at the time, that loving connection was all I needed. I have always wished him happiness, and I believe he found it, just not with me. To this day, I have not forgotten him. I have kept all of his photos, and his painting still hangs on my wall.

Later in life, I tried to find him again. I wrote his story for a publication and reached out through an Italian-speaking friend of a friend. There were many men named Luigi, and contacting each one was a painstaking process. One man said he wished he were my Luigi! Eventually, I found one Luigi who had died shortly before we could connect. I felt he was the one I had loved and lost. His family was uncomfortable talking about it, but they hinted that perhaps someday they might consider sharing more. My questions about him were never answered.

From this, I have learned that love endures beyond time and is everlasting in ways we cannot always understand, and that some losses stay with us forever, shaping who we are and how we see the world.

My plan is to go back to Rapallo and revisit those beloved places, the ones that marked the beginning of my journey into independence. That was where my love for solo travel adventures started, and even now, after all these years, it hasn't ended. I often think of Luigi, my sweet Luigi, and hope he lived a good life, filled with happiness and peace.

When the time came for him to return to Italy, both of us knew it was the end of our romantic chapter. I was preparing to move to Canada, chasing a new dream of a better life with my family. Luigi was a devout Catholic, and it was clear he would be expected to marry within his faith. We shared a tearful farewell; the ache of that moment still lingers in my mind.

At that time, I was working three jobs, morning, evening, and weekends, just to save enough money to emigrate. My life was a whirlwind of routines, sacrifices, and hope. That beautiful romance had come and gone, yet he had the most profound impact on me. I often wonder if he kept my photos, tucked away somewhere, memories of a girl who once meant everything to him.

He was a remarkable, beautiful person, and I feel so fortunate to have met him. He transformed me from a broken-hearted girl into a woman who discovered her confidence again, as well as the courage to travel alone. That first solo trip was a turning point in my life – a leap of faith that opened so many doors.

To date, I have taken 80 solo journeys, each one transformed and defined who I am. Interestingly, I've never met another Luigi, not since that first love. Truly, he was one of a kind. I am grateful to carry his love in my heart all these years. He set me free.

Because of him, I changed. He gave me the precious gifts of confidence and self-esteem, helping me piece myself back together after my broken engagement. Meeting Luigi was an achingly beautiful chapter in my coming-of-age season. Thank you, Luigi, for putting me back together. I love you.

216

CHAPTER 27

Goodbye England, Hello Canada

Around the time we entered a major life transition by deciding to leave England and emigrate to another country, my brother Alan got engaged to a girl named Tina from the nearby Girls' High School. I often found myself watching Tina stand alone outside her grandmother's small, round house at Wivenhoe Park, a quiet figure simply lingering there as if lost in thought. Her parents were not present, and her grandmother raised her single-handedly.

Little did I know then that Tina would impact our lives in ways I couldn't imagine.

When Alan first brought her to our home, it struck me how little she talked and how she kept her eyes cast down, as if she didn't want to attract attention. She carried a gentle, modest air; her demeanour was always demure and reserved. I remember feeling that her shy silence revealed more than any conversation ever could, as if she were hiding something. I sensed she had a dark secret and a shadow side that I only understood much later.

Her guarded gaze was perhaps a hint of her own story.

When the boys in the village heard about Alan's engagement, their conversations plainly showed their judgment and crude curiosity:

"Joy, I hear Alan has got engaged to that girl."

"Who, Tina?"

"Yes, her, that one. Do you know we've all had sex with her? We call her the Village Bike."

I kept these harsh words to myself, though they stung. Alan was completely besotted with her, talked about her all the time. I didn't like her, felt she was shifty; no real eye contact, always avoiding, always silent. I didn't trust her, but I kept my thoughts to myself.

Meanwhile, we still dreamed of moving to Canada. Even Tina, Alan's fiancée, was joining us and shared in those hopes.

To save up, I took on an extra weekend job working at different racecourses around the county. The money was good, better than I'd ever earned before. I went with a group of girls from the Lathe Company. We made money on the Tote, which involved betting on horse races through a pool betting system, and winnings were calculated based on predicting race outcomes and the total number of successful bettors. We made decent money on race days. We worked Saturdays and Sundays, which meant long but rewarding days.

My very good friend Joyce Munson had arranged everything and recruited us, making it feel like a fun adventure rather than just work. Not too long after, Joyce asked me to be her bridesmaid when she got married and I was honoured to be a part of her special day.

Joy at her friend Joyce's wedding in 1957.

Joy with Joyce Munson and friends at the racetrack.

In the evenings, I bartended at local pubs, bringing in even more money. It felt good, the kind of work that kept the future in sight. I was saving hard, every penny, toward a new life. Over the past year, we started saving seriously. We were considering three countries: New Zealand, Australia, and Canada. We researched the requirements for all three countries and eventually decided on Canada. The other countries offered free transport, but we had to work in the jobs they assigned us for two years. We decided we would like to find our own jobs; therefore, we all saved for the transportation costs.

Before we emigrated, we made arrangements for Alan to move ahead of us and find a place to stay, so that when we arrived, we would have a roof over our heads. Ian and his wife had already left earlier to settle in.

All this time, I was juggling three jobs, leaving little room for dating or much of a social life. Still, I went out occasionally. I continued working in these three roles through 1956 and 1957, and into 1958, until it was closer to leaving.

By 1958, mum and I were busy preparing for the journey to Canada in September. There was so much to sort through, so much to get rid of. Our landlord said we could leave the furniture because the house wouldn't be rented again. Anything left inside would be destroyed once the house was torn down.

We faced limitations on what we could take with us. It was a difficult choice, deciding what was really necessary. I've often thought back on that time and marvelled at how much I learned about patience and sacrifice. We wanted a new start, but leaving behind the familiar was not easy. Still, I understood that sometimes you had to let go of what you loved to reach for what you hoped for.

I remember the day I had to let go of my bike. It had been more than just a mode of transportation to work; it was a faithful friend that carried me through good days and bad. My bond with it was simple but deep.

During that time, we barely saw much of Alan's fiancée, Tina. She kept to herself, was painfully shy, and hardly answered our questions when we did see her. She was tall and slender, always dressed with a kind of effortless elegance that made you notice her even when she wished to go unnoticed. Dark hair framed her face, and dark eyes seemed clouded with complicated feelings. Despite my attempts to reach out, her lack of words made her seem distant, almost cold, and I learned that sometimes people ward off kindness because they are afraid or unsure how to truly accept it. So our relationship was always cool, at best.

Mum and I worked tirelessly that year, trying to save every penny as the days and months passed in a blur of work. We de-cluttered our home, sold what we could, and hunted for cheap suitcases. The plan was to travel by train to Southampton, the three of us plus my dog Nicki, who was as much a part of the family as anyone. We hardly spoke about our unspoken fears about the move: what if we didn't like our new home? What if it was a mistake to move?

After we arrived in Montreal, we would take the train to Vancouver. We pored over maps and pondered our memories of England, knowing that everything familiar was about to change.

September 6th arrived faster than I ever imagined. Tina had come the day before, clutching her single suitcase, silently. We woke early, shared tea and toast as if every moment might be the last. We washed the utensils, tidied the house, and left the key carefully inside on the table. Every move had meaning and was weighted by sadness and nostalgia.

Then we walked to the train station, heavy-hearted but resolute. Nicki, my darling dog, had to go in the guard's van. He had to be tied up in the van throughout the trip and he hated it. I kept him company there along with the suitcases, feeling a quiet ache as I watched him and feeling sorry for him. We transferred trains at Colchester and then in London, from Liverpool Street to King's Cross, and each time Nicki was bundled into crowded spaces. My heart ached for Nicki's discomfort.

From the guard's van, I saw little of the countryside rushing past because I didn't want to leave Nicki alone as I could see his little face full of confusion and distress at being tied up. I wished I could hold him close, keep him safe from every hurt.

When we finally reached Southampton, the docks were a cacophony of noise, people, and movement. It was chaos, yet somehow we found our ship, the QSS Arkadia. That vessel would take us across the vast Atlantic to the eastern shores of Canada. Our new beginning.

Mum had our papers ready. I was told Nicki had to stay in a kennel on the upper deck, near the huge funnel that sounded the horn. It broke my heart to think he would be alone up there. I carried him up there reluctantly, my own tears falling as I placed him in that tiny cage. He cried out, and I felt a pain in my chest at the thought of him feeling scared. I knew somehow that I would find a way to sneak him down into my cabin, even if that meant facing punishment.

When we found our cabin on the ship, it was simply a small space with three bunk beds pressed against the walls. Mum claimed the bottom bunk, I took the top, and Tina chose the one opposite us on the other side of the room. It all sounds straightforward now, but at the time, it was anything but that. I remember feeling an overwhelming wave of stress. More than anything, I was truly sorry to leave England behind. Mum, on the other hand, was glad to be leaving, eager for a new start. However, within a year, she would return to England to live with Colin and his family, never settling in Canada as we had hoped.

Honestly, I was heartbroken to be leaving everything familiar. Despite the difficulties and hardships we faced, I couldn't help but feel a profound sense of loss. I was leaving all my friends behind. I remember crying all the way to the ship, sniffling and feeling devastated as if my whole world was crumbling. To leave behind everything I knew for an uncertain future was terrifying, and I had no guarantees that life would be better there. I wondered if I would find a job, make friends, and fall in love again. All I knew about Canada was what I had read, that they spoke the same language, or close enough. But that didn't make it any easier.

As we went through the process of checking our suitcases, emptying them, and putting away our things for the seven-day ship journey, my mind was a chaotic mess. I hoped Tina would be talkative and lively on the journey, but she said nothing. She seemed almost indifferent, as if going or staying made no difference to her.

Why was I such an emotional wreck while she remained so calm and collected? Mum was excited, her face lit up with anticipation. It was not her first time on an ocean liner; she had traveled with my father to places like China, Egypt, and India. Her experience made her more familiar with change, I suppose. But I felt I had lost control and was frightened of the unknown.

We found the dining room and our table after changing and freshening up. There was a dance scheduled, and a cheerful German boy asked me to dance. We had to balance an orange between our foreheads, which was harder than it looked, but we managed to laugh through it. It was a fun night filled with simple joy and that lifted my mood. We didn't stay long; eventually, mum and I went to bed. We couldn't see Tina and were concerned about her, but we knew she had a key, so we settled down.

Joy dancing on the QSS Arkadia en route to
Canada from England in September 1958.

A photo taken of Joy on the upper deck of QSS Arkadia in 1958.

As the ship set sail from Southampton into the Atlantic Ocean, I watched the shoreline fade away. The water was surprisingly smooth at first, and the blue skies had perfectly formed clouds floating by.

But that calm would not last.

In the morning, mum and I noticed that Tina's bed had not been slept in. We went to breakfast, and then I went up to see Nicki, our little dog, to feed him and walk him around the deck. Mum came too. Up on deck, the breeze was strong and invigorating, and Nicki was so grateful to see us that he whined and squirmed with delight. I suspect he thought we had abandoned him. We stayed a little while, and I tucked him into my coat for warmth and comfort, sneaking him back down to our cabin for a rest. Mum was feeling unwell from the motion. Her face was pale and strained, so I carefully placed Nicki into my bunk and stayed nearby for a while.

I worried then that she might get seasick, so I set out to find if there was a medical office on board to get her some relief. I couldn't leave Nicki alone for long because he might bark or cause trouble, so I had to sneak him into the kennel when I went to find the medical centre.

On the way back down to the main deck, I saw Tina with a group of men, their arms closely draped around her. I was shocked. But I remembered what the boys from the village had told me about her, and now I could see that it was all true. We never saw her sleeping in our cabin during the entire voyage. Mum was disgusted, and I had a feeling about what was really going on, but said nothing. She was supposed to be marrying my brother, Alan, and was wearing his ring, but I guess that didn't matter much to her.

The boys from the village had told me she had been with all of them. Now it seemed she was indiscriminately sleeping with anyone and everyone on board. At the time, I wasn't sure what we were supposed to tell him, if anything at all.

Mum got terribly seasick and stayed in the cabin for the rest of the voyage. I just kept going about my routines, eating the meals served to us, walking the dog whenever I could, watching the guitar players on deck, and taking part in the games in the lounge. I brought my mother her meals, but she wasn't really interested in eating, though I made sure she got some soup and her sea-sickness medication.

It wasn't only mum who was sick on that ship. Our voyage took place during the upheaval of the Hungarian Revolution, and refugees were everywhere, some sleeping on the decks, others lounging in chairs, all looking sickly and exhausted. You could see the worry shadowing their faces, yet I sensed some hope for their new life in Canada as well.

We didn't see Tina in the cabin again until it was time to pack up and disembark. Mum was too weak to help, so I did what I could, helping her pack and get cleaned up. We slowly made our way toward the disembarking area, standing in line to set foot into Canada. It felt like crossing a line into a new world, yet carrying many of the old fears with us.

Once ashore, we found a taxi to the train station. The train to Vancouver was waiting, and I was excited and nervous at once. It turned out to be a long, slow ride across the country to the West Coast of Canada, the landscape rolling past the window in endless shades of green and brown with some mountains sprinkled in. I was overjoyed when I saw a vending machine on the platform, and I couldn't help but smile at the simple thrill of buying a chocolate bar from it. It was something I'd never seen before. These new things seemed small at the time, but marked our tentative steps toward a new life.

The train had bunks and shared bathrooms. Nicki, our dog, had to be secured in the guard's van. I was told I could walk him at each stop. He was quite panicky about being tied up and separated from me, so I made it a point to visit him often, to get him off the train whenever we stopped. It is so important to care for those who depend on us, even in small ways.

Vancouver finally appeared in the distance. When we reached the final station, I could feel the unknown pressing down on me. The crowd was thick, suitcases and bags around us, my dog, Nicki, trembling at my side. Mum looked a bit pale, even though her seasickness had eased. She was still weak from not eating enough.

Then, through the crowd came Alan, walking steadily towards us. He hugged Tina, but didn't seem to notice mum or me. Instead, he announced that a car was waiting to take us to a new house.

So we set off with Alan, his arm around Tina, heading into our new beginning. Everything was happening so fast, and I wondered what our life would be like in Vancouver, Canada. Despite my grief at leaving my friends behind in England, I held onto the hope that better days would come.

CHAPTER 28

West Vancouver

My brother rented a house on Balaclava Street in West Vancouver. It was a semi-detached place with a basement and a small porch out front. The main level had a living room, a dining room, one bedroom, a tiny kitchen, and a bathroom. I wondered where we would all sleep, but it didn't take long to figure it out. Alan gave Tina the main bedroom beside the bathroom and said he'd sleep on the sofa in the living room.

Mum asked, "Where are we sleeping?"

"In the basement," he said.

We followed him down the short stairs to the lower level. He showed us a small room with two single beds, each with a little chest of drawers next to it for our clothes. There was no bathroom down there, so we had to go upstairs whenever we needed to wash or use the toilet.

I was secretly furious about this setup.

It seemed clear to me that it was arranged so he could have easy access to Tina. I think mum suspected the same. She knew about Tina's behaviour on the ship and was probably thinking the same way I was. We believed it was best for Alan to discover Tina's behaviour himself, as he would not have listened to our warnings.

These living arrangements didn't last very long.

Since we didn't have jobs yet and Alan was the only one working, he did the shopping because he had a car. He worked at the Catholic Children's Aid Society and played in a musical trio. Mum took care of the cooking.

There was a landline phone in the house, paid for by Alan. I thought I'd need it once I started applying for jobs, which I planned to do quickly. I was eager to earn money as soon as I could. But I didn't have any proper clothes for job interviews. I had a blue corduroy dress with a gold stripe, tweed pants, and an orange polka dot skirt I made myself back in England. The trunk my mom had used in the Anderson shelter had been shipped with us, but hadn't arrived yet. I had filled it with my clothes.

I found out where to register for a job and, dressed in my casual corduroy dress, went to sign up and get my social insurance number (SIN). When I arrived and was called in, I explained my experience to the woman at the desk and stressed I needed to start working right away. She looked me over and said, "You're not dressed appropriately for a business office."

Her open disapproval made me feel humiliated.

I replied, "It takes a while for our clothes to catch up with us. We only got here yesterday."

I had hoped that registering immediately for work would demonstrate my eagerness to start as soon as possible. She didn't seem impressed, but she did provide me with a name and a phone number to call for an interview. I took the bus home and was thrilled to find our trunk had arrived, so that I had a change of clothes.

I got a job at J. Arthur Rank Film Distributors and began working right away. My boss was a very nice man who showed me the ropes when I started working. It was interesting work. We supplied the films for the local cinemas. I had grown up loving movies and had once dreamed of becoming a continuity girl and working on films, so it felt like a good fit.

It might have been, except for one staff member who decided I was a special delicacy. After a few weeks, I looked for another job and found one with the Chubb Safe Company. I had another good boss, who gave me raises when I earned them.

Things were going well at work. I was paid enough to give a significant amount of money to my mum. I even opened an account at a dress shop to upgrade my wardrobe.

I was amazed by the mountains and trees in British Columbia. It was so breathtaking. I signed up for a couple of ski lessons on Grouse Mountain for the following Saturday. I'd have to rent boots and skis, but I was willing to give it a go. It seemed entirely different from anything I knew, but since I was here in BC and there was a baby hill just for beginners like me, I figured I had nothing to lose. I'd give it a shot and see how it went. After just arriving in Vancouver, I was open to trying anything new and excited about skiing. Thankfully, I had fun on the slopes.

About seven months after we emigrated to Canada, around April 1959, I was enjoying my job at the Chubb Safe Company and appreciated my cheerful colleagues. I still felt happy while trying to overcome my homesickness. However, things back home in Balaclava weren't going as smoothly.

Tina had given our house phone number to the guys she had "consorted" with on the ship. They called her a lot to talk. At the time, Alan was busy performing and traveling to different gigs, so he was gone most of the time. Mum and I understood what was happening, but how does one tell Alan the truth when he wasn't willing to hear a negative word about Tina?

It all seemed like it was heading for a big, crashing finale!

On the same day I had scheduled my ski lesson on the baby hill, Tina told me we'd both been invited to a chalet party on Grouse Mountain.

"I have a ski lesson that day," I said.

"I think the baby hill is close to the chalet," she replied. "Come after your lesson."

"Who will be there?" I asked.

"The Ski Patrol guys are throwing the party. The chalet belongs to their parents, but they let the kids use it sometimes."

"I'll see how my lesson goes and if I can find the place, I'll come. I need to know what time the gondola stops running so I don't get stuck up there. My lesson ends quite late," I said.

"Okay, I'm going to the party," she said matter-of-factly.

The day of my lesson finally arrived. I spent the morning with my mother, then put on my warm pants and a sweater before heading up to the mountain. I wore some moccasins to change into after the lesson, since I was planning to rent boots and skis. I figured I would take the gondola down and catch the bus home afterwards.

The lesson went pretty much as I expected. I knew I'd never be a skier, but I had fun trying to stay upright on the little hill. The instructor knew I wasn't going to be a pro, but he helped me enjoy trying to keep my balance on skis. I realized this was just a one-time thing, and the look on the instructor's face told me all I needed to know about my future in skiing.

When my hour was up, I swapped my boots and skis for my moccasins and walked the short distance to the chalet. I knocked, went inside, and saw a group of young men and women gathered around.

Food and drink were laid out on a table, and I helped myself to a glass of juice and a bit of salad. I was hungry after the lesson on the baby hill. I found a vacant chair and sat down to eat. Most of the others were drinking wine or liquor. I hadn't had much experience with either before, so it was all new to me. I sipped my juice slowly.

Outside, it was starting to get dark. I wondered how everyone would get down the mountain once the gondola shut down. I guessed they were planning to stay overnight. I didn't know when the gondola would close, but I was feeling a little anxious about it. I was new to everything – the ski crowd, the mountain, the country – and I was feeling my way around slowly. I had no idea what to expect, and I knew I had no ride home once the lift stopped running.

My heart sank when I saw Tina with a boy I didn't know. I wasn't sure how to handle it, seeing her with other boys while she was engaged to Alan.

Suddenly, the lights in the chalet went out.

I jumped in fear and whispered to the guy sitting next to me, "What's going on?"

"Now we get to have some fun," he said.

"What kind of fun?" I whispered.

"Sex, with anyone you want or everyone you want," he laughed. I gasped in horror.

"No, not me, I can't do that," I said.

I could hear moans and orgasms around me, so I shot up, grabbed my purse, headed for the door, opened it, and stepped outside into the snow. Luckily, it had been worn down by the many tracks left by people. I was wearing moccasins that weren't meant for snow, but panic pushed me to keep going.

The lift lights were out, so I started walking, heading down until I reached the spot where I had taken the lift earlier that day. I made my way to a bus stop and waited for a bus that would take me close to our place. The bus dropped me off about a block away, and I walked to the house and rang the bell. I hadn't brought a key because I wasn't sure about security on the mountain while I was skiing. I felt relieved to see mum open the door.

I was crying and wondering if that kind of date night was normal in Canada. Mum sat me down, helped calm me, and made some hot chocolate. My feet were soaked and freezing. She brought me a towel and warm socks while I sipped the hot chocolate. I told her all about it, including that Tina was there with a boy and behaving inappropriately with him.

"I doubt we will see her tonight," I said. Mum was not surprised. She told me she had got up one night and caught Tina having sex with a strange man on the sofa in the living room.

Alan was away that night, singing with his band, and was due back the next morning. I went to bed, feeling emotionally drained.

The next morning, Alan came home and his first question was, "Where's Tina?"

I hadn't said anything about her inappropriate behaviour up to that point. I was mad that mum had seen her and had witnessed her actions on the ship and in the house, so I responded, "The last time I saw her, she was in a Chalet on Grouse Mountain. I heard a hotel mentioned, so maybe that's where she is with her boyfriends."

He got really angry then and called me a few choice names. He blamed me for her behaviour. I was shocked by his accusation, but I knew he was feeling deeply hurt. Mum, who never made a fuss, chipped in and told him we hadn't seen her in our cabin on the ship and that she herself had seen her having sex with a man on that sofa in our living room.

He was furious, red with rage.

"Which hotel?" he asked.

"Georgia hotel, I think, that's where they usually hang out," I said.

He stormed into the bedroom and cleared out all her belongings – clothes, toiletries, everything she owned was in that room. He packed it all into her suitcase, then roared out of the house, got into his car, and drove away.

About an hour later, he came back alone. He put his hand into his pocket, pulled out the engagement ring, and placed it on the table.

Mum and I didn't say a word, and Alan went into the bedroom and slammed the door.

That wasn't the end of her, but it definitely marked the end of any skiing I might have wanted to do in the future.

A few days later, I received an account statement from the dress shop where I had opened an account. The invoice was overdue, and I knew I hadn't purchased any of those items. When I called the store to ask about it, the owner told me, "Your friend bought them and said you gave her permission to use your account." I told her that I had not authorized anyone to use my account. I was furious.

I knew where Tina worked. She was a teller at a bank in the city centre. The next day, during my lunch hour, I went to the bank and stood in line in front of her teller station. She looked startled to see me, but stayed quiet.

I laid the invoice on the counter and said, "Here, this invoice belongs to you. You lied and bought clothes charged to my account. You can pay for this. It's your responsibility."

She had some nerve. This was before credit cards were common. I thought that, at the very least, the store should have called me first to check if I had authorised her. I walked out of the bank, and I never heard from the dress shop again, so I guess she paid her bill.

That was the last I saw of her. I didn't miss her then, and I never have since.

CHAPTER 29

A New Beginning

The house was much quieter without Tina's drama. Alan moved into Tina's old bedroom. He was also thinking about moving to Ontario, where the music scene was stronger.

My mum was looking after my dog Nicki while I worked. She was in her sixties, and I was worried about her. She seemed extremely lonely and homesick for England. When Alan was touring, she was alone during the day with just the dog for company. She had always been a cat person, and looking back, I believe she wished for a furry feline to curl up with, as well as all for the company of her grandchildren and old friends from England.

One day during my lunch break, I was walking along when I saw a woman standing on a street corner holding a leaflet. People hurried past her without paying any attention.

As I got closer, I realized it was my mother. I called out, "Mum, what are you doing? Those Jehovah's Witnesses have gotten to you. You shouldn't answer the door to them; they're trying to recruit you." I tore up the leaflet.

She explained, "Two nice young women came to the door and I invited them in. We had a nice chat. They asked me if I would help them out by doing this."

"It's okay, mum. Let's get you home," I said, and I took her to the bus stop. I waited until her bus arrived. As she got on, I told her, "I'll see if I can get off work early today." I was starting to really worry about her.

When I returned to work, I asked if I could leave early. My boss agreed, and I hurried to the bus stop, eager to get home. When I arrived, I found mum preparing supper, peeling potatoes into a bowl of water at the sink.

I called out, "I'm home."

When she turned around, I could see she had been crying. I went to her and asked, "Oh mum, what's wrong?" as I hugged her.

She looked unhappy and said, "I'm so homesick. I want to go home. There's nothing for me here. I feel lonely and bored. I miss my sister, Colin, and the grandchildren. I want to go back."

She started crying then, her tears flowing freely as if her heart was breaking, and she wiped her eyes on her apron. I had never seen mum cry before, not even during the war when things were tough, so I knew she must be very unhappy to be crying like that. I didn't know how to help her then. She didn't have any money, and her pension hadn't started yet.

I said, "Let me think about it. I'm homesick too, but we came here for a reason, mum. What would you go back to?"

She explained that Colin had written to say she could stay with him and his family and help with the foster children. Colin and Paddy were fostering children in Liverpool at that time, in addition to their own three kids.

I wondered how I could make her wish come true. This was around April 1959.

I had been dating Mike for a couple of months. I met him on a blind date set up by my brother Alan. He had spent some time in Boston before coming to Canada and attended MIT, the Massachusetts Institute of Technology, while he was there. We hit it off on our first date, and he asked me every day to marry him.

I had planned to set a wedding date, but hadn't done so at that point. After an emotional talk with my mother, and knowing deep down that she would be returning to England, I talked to Mike. We decided to get married sooner rather than later, so mum could come to my wedding before she went back. He kindly offered to dip into his savings to pay for her fare to Liverpool.

We bought her a ticket for late May 1959, when she would sail back to England. I wouldn't see her again until 1963. I told her we would arrange for her to go back to Colin and his family after we got married. She was incredibly happy to hear this, and also that she would see me get married. As it turned out, she had attended Ian's wedding to Babs while we were living in England, but Colin got married without telling her until after the fact. He and his wife then turned up to live with us, which was a surprise. I was glad she would see me get married. It would be years before Alan married Martha, and that turned out to be a disaster.

Joy's painting of her wedding day photo

Joy and her mother.

Mike and Joy on their wedding day
on May 9th 1959.

We began planning our wedding. Mike came from a Catholic family. I think he probably knew how his mother might react to him marrying a Protestant. We bought a simple gold ring for the ceremony. It would be another two years before I received a lovely engagement ring and a wide gold band. I eventually mounted the engagement ring onto the band. It was stunning.

Mike first went to a Catholic church to ask about getting married. When the priest learned he was marrying a Protestant, he suggested that he might find a nice Catholic girl instead. That was a taste of what was to come.

We contacted the United Church in Kitsilano. The reverend there agreed to marry us, so we set the date for May 9th. It was going to be a simple white wedding. Mike's friend was his best man, and I had a friend from work who was my bridesmaid. Alan gave me away. He was already making plans to move to Ontario for his singing career.

For our honeymoon, we kept things simple and drove down to Oregon in a borrowed car, staying in Seaside and Cannon Beach, Oregon. It was magnificent to spend time by the ocean.

After our honeymoon, we moved into a flat on 4th Avenue in Vancouver and stayed there for a few months. The house was up for sale, and real estate agents kept knocking on our door, eager to view our furnished place. We didn't always let them in. We shared a bathroom with a man who lived in another flat on the same floor. One evening, I went to use the bathroom, turned on the light, and found our neighbour in the tub, sitting in the dark. I quickly shut the door and called out, "You might want to lock the door."

During the few months we lived on 4th Avenue, we always went camping on the weekends. Mike had bought a sedan delivery van and knew all the parks where we could camp. I remember visiting Manning Park and being struck by the devastating damage from forest fires. There was a sign in the park that stated, 'The one who started this should also be hanged,' and it showed a cigarette hanging from a chain.

Unfortunately, people still start fires in Canada's beautiful forests. During the drought season, many fires burn in British Columbia and other provinces.

Every weekend in 1959, we went to a different park, either in Canada or the United States. My dog Nicki loved romping in the woods during these trips. We visited parks in British Columbia, Washington, Oregon, Idaho, Montana, Nevada, California, Arizona, Colorado, and Utah. We stayed longer at Yosemite, Yellowstone, and the Grand Canyon. Camping near the edge of the Grand Canyon was pretty frightening, with lightning streaking across the sky and thunder rumbling all around.

While camping in Yellowstone Park, I had a scary run-in with a big bear while I was frying up some delicious canned bacon over an open fire. It was pretty scary. Mike was chopping wood nearby, and I ran over to him, still clutching the frying pan.

He yelled, "Drop the bacon!" so I tossed the pan over my shoulder, hoping the bear would go for the bacon instead of me.

I was shaken up. That night, we slept in the car. To our surprise, the car rocked during the night when a bear stood up with its paws on top of the roof. The bear was probably just looking for food. In the morning, the tent was torn apart. We couldn't help but think about what might've happened if we'd been sleeping inside like we usually do. I shuddered at the thought!

There was a strict rule about not feeding bears in the parks; however, many folks ignored it and were fined. On the drive home, we saw bears begging for food and people offering it through their car windows. Folks, these are wild animals – they need to find their own food. If bears get used to being fed or become a nuisance, they're usually put down. It's best to leave them alone.

One weekend, we returned to the flat to find our bed rumpled up and a pair of women's underwear on the bed. We knew then it was time to move out and find a place where we'd have privacy. We found an apartment in another house on York Avenue. It had a lovely view of the English Bay, with its sparkling waters, and the majestic mountains towering in the distance, their peaks capped with snow. In this apartment, we shared a fridge with another tenant. We had a small kitchen, living room, and bedroom.

The landlady wasn't too keen on having a dog, but she agreed as long as we kept him quiet and made sure he didn't make a mess in the apartment. Nicki was a good dog and completely house-trained. We kept traveling on weekends or during longer summer holidays. We lived there for a year.

Just after our second Christmas at York Avenue, I started feeling ill and Mike offered to walk Nicki. Nicki was terrified of all men and didn't want to go with him. Unfortunately, Nicki suddenly broke away from Mike during the walk, ran into the road, and was hit by a car. Mike carried him back home. I could see from his swelling and unsteady walk that he had internal bleeding. He couldn't control his bowels and ended up making a mess in the apartment.

I called a vet and had to have Nicki put down. I was heartbroken over losing him. He was eight years old. He had always been a very timid dog. Looking back now, I would never again put an animal through the conditions he endured to travel to Canada with me.

We cleaned the apartment, but the landlady still asked us to move. We were ready and happy to leave. One day, I caught her with her eye to the keyhole when I had opened the door suddenly, so I knew she was being nosy. She was not keen on us having company either.

Mike was trying his hand at brewing beer while we lived there. It was horrible stuff, but his mates who played in the Irish Soccer team with him lapped it up – not literally from a bowl, but they thought it was nectar. I did tell him this was a one-off to brew beer at home, and that the next place we moved to would have no beer bottles brewing behind the sofa.

We were quite active socially back then. Besides camping trips with another couple, we belonged to the WISE Club in Vancouver, which included Welsh, Irish, Scottish, and English members. We enjoyed many of their community events, especially dinners and dances. People dressed up for everything then, so it was always special to get out our best clothes, wear a nice dress, and have an evening filled with fun. My husband also played soccer with the Irish Club, and in his youth, he even played professionally in England.

In early 1961, we found a furnished apartment on Second Avenue. The building managers, a lovely couple, were very kind; they often baked goodies and shared them with us.

Mike was feeling a bit stuck at his job. He was a metallurgist, focusing on stainless steel. When the Second Narrows Bridge collapsed in 1958, he was called as an expert witness to help figure out why. A Royal Commission later said the collapse happened because of a miscalculation by the bridge engineers. Nineteen people lost their lives in the collapse. The bridge was eventually rebuilt and renamed the Memorial Bridge.

Mike was full of knowledge and wanted to move forward in his career. He applied to steel companies across Canada and the U.S. Finally, he got a job as a Senior Metallurgist at Atlas Steels in Welland, Ontario, starting in August 1961.

We began planning our move. We decided to drive through the United States to get to Ontario. That meant saying goodbye to British Columbia, as we packed up the car and headed toward Seattle for our journey across the U.S. We had a big map spread out and a week to make the trip before Mike was due to start his new job. British Columbia had given us many memories – some good, some bad. Now we wondered what Ontario had in store for us. We set off with a light, expectant heart, thinking about new beginnings and new places to explore along the way.

During the more than two years in Vancouver, I had already said goodbye to my mother and Nicki. I couldn't help wondering what this next chapter would bring. Fortunately, by this time, I held a quiet understanding that every ending is simply a prelude to a new beginning.

Dear reader, more about my next chapter in life is in the next book. Stay tuned!

Epilogue

Looking back on a life that has spanned nearly a century, I see how each season has moulded my soul. This is the end of one life story but also the beginning of another, far removed from the familiar lands of England and Scotland, where my roots are deeply planted.

We left England with hearts full of hope, believing we were moving towards a better life, though none of us truly understood what that entailed at the time. We carried dreams wrapped in longing and uncertainty, as if life itself were an unfolding mystery waiting to be explored. I remember the quiet hope we carried, despite the darkness we sometimes faced and the fear that it might be extinguished by life's trials and tribulations.

Personally, I was not sorry to leave the old row house where I had spent fifteen years, but leaving England was a different matter. That country was the only home I had ever known, its weather and streets woven into my very soul and my war-scarred childhood. I mourned the loss of relatives, friends, familiar sights and sounds, the comforting rhythm of daily life there.

I held a deep wish inside me for a home I could be proud of, one that radiated warmth and hospitality. A home I could invite friends to. I yearned for a space I could call my own, free from the shame of cockroaches, spiders and mice scurrying in the shadows. I longed for inside plumbing, a private bathroom and toilet, a beautiful home where I could rest without external hardships.

I dreamed of a job that would afford me the opportunity to decorate my beautiful home with colours that reflected my spirit, and to have a kitchen with modern appliances so I could learn to cook and bring joy to those around me. I also imagined laundry days made easier by a washing machine and dryer, instead of heating water on a gas ring and scrubbing in outdoor tubs or trudging to public baths.

To me, possessing such comfort would be like reaching a piece of heaven. I often wondered how long it would take to achieve these simple yet meaningful dreams. A fierce determination grew within me to find work quickly, to toil relentlessly until I achieved what my aching heart longed for. I vowed never again to be hungry, dirty, or scruffy. I hoped this new life in Canada would be the key to those promises I made to myself.

I kept my dreams close, whispering them softly to avoid jinxing my hopes by speaking them aloud. I was convinced I was not alone in longing for a better future while harbouring a lasting love for the country I was leaving behind. I belonged to that quiet, determined group of souls who carried a bittersweet love; nostalgia intertwined with longing.

Over the years, I made countless return visits, each one a journey through memory, tears and laughter. Deciding which side of the ocean feels like home is a long process, often with both places claiming real estate in my heart. Even now, although Canada is where I reside and find happiness, I hold a gentle wish for one more trip to the land I still consider the home of my heart.

Looking back with the wisdom of age, I see that life is a delicate balancing act between love and loss, hope and acceptance, pain and healing. Every challenge taught me resilience, every trial and goodbye deepened my understanding of what it means to overcome and truly belong.

That childhood of hardship and longing taught me lessons I carry to this day about perseverance, about the enduring power of dreams, and the importance of cherishing the roots that sustain us no matter where life takes us.

Love and hugs,
Joy Elise Fox
November 2025

Acknowledgements

When I committed myself to writing this book, I soon realized how much hard work it truly was. I had thought it would be simple to just sit and pick my brain for this memoir, but it turned out to be more than I bargained for. I often left it unfinished; sometimes because life threw distractions my way, and other times because my head would throb with the dull ache of remembering, making it too hard to focus. Yet, I always found my way back to it, and I'm glad I did. Looking back now, I see how much those moments of pouring my memories onto the page meant to me.

My mother was the first person who encouraged me to write. I was a shy girl, too timid to speak up often, so putting my thoughts on paper was a much easier way to express myself. Writing became a habit, something I did regularly, almost instinctively. I owe her a great deal for that gift. I wish she were here now so she could read these words. Wherever you are, mum, I want to send you my loving thanks. For your ongoing encouragement throughout your life and mine: your support still lives on in my heart.

My children have all found their own ways to embrace writing, in different forms. Melody has dedicated herself to medical articles and presentations, sharing her knowledge. April was a wonderful writer of essays when she was young, and she even wrote children's books. Steven has been a writer throughout his career as well, and he published a book. I remember when he helped me with technical matters, showing me how to use online resources when I was struggling to write a couple of e-books a few years ago. I think I can say that my love of writing has somehow rubbed off on my children, and I'm proud of that.

Many friends have asked me over the years when I would finish this book. Each time, I felt their encouragement deep in my heart. Well, now I can say I've finally finished it. And I want all of you – my friends, my writing groups, everyone who has ever supported me – to read it. It's a bit of my life, after all.

A huge thanks must go to Sylvia Yu Friedman. She found me at a time when I had written the last words and was standing at the edge of what's next. Her guidance has been invaluable through the editing, printing, and marketing stages. Thank you for all the Zoom calls, the interviews, and the suggestions you have given that helped shape this book.

I feel so honoured to have someone like you to work with. You have done an amazing editing job. Each time I have read your edits, I was filled with admiration for your talent.

Thank you, Sylvia, from the bottom of my heart, for helping me turn this dream into a reality. I am thrilled.

If you'd like to contact Joy for speaking engagements
or media interviews, please email:

Sylvia@epictalesmedia.com